Praise

'I expected a book about getting speaker. What I got was a deep di ...nat actually makes a speaker commercially viable, from positioning and bookability to marketing and industry realities. It exceeded my expectations because it wasn't just fluff or generic public speaking tips. Maria takes a clear stance on what works, what doesn't, and why so many speakers fail. That's refreshing. My kind of book!'
— **David Newman**, CSP and 3× best-selling author of *Do It! Speaking* and *Do It! Selling*

'Fantastic! Selfishly I wish this was written five plus years ago. It would have saved me so much time.'
— **Brendan Hall**, speaker and round-the-world yachtsman

'This is a refreshingly honest and practical guide to what truly makes a speaker commercially successful. Maria cuts through the fluff with humour and clarity, delivering hard-earned insights that every speaker needs to hear. Essential reading for building a thriving, sustainable speaking business – and like having mini Maria in your pocket!'
— **Captain Emma** Henderson MBE, professional speaker, airline pilot, charity founder and CEO

'This book is a game changer for any speaker who wants to grow their speaking business and get booked again and again and again! Maria's Bookability Formula is brilliant in its simplicity yet underpinned by a wealth of insights and wisdom acquired from decades of working within the speaking industry.'
— **Mary Tillson-Wharton**, keynote speaker coach, expert in corporate messaging and Verbal Behaviour Intelligence

'A must-read for speakers at any stage, whether you're just starting out or already running a successful speaking business. This book is packed with relevant, practical insights you can use.'
— **Jamil Qureshi**, TEDx speaker, performance coach, facilitator, entrepreneur, and author

'Maria has distilled decades of experience into a practical, no-nonsense guide that every speaker, whether aspiring or seasoned, needs to read. *The Bookability Formula* isn't just about getting on stage; it's about staying in demand, commanding higher fees and turning speaking into a thriving business. Essential reading for anyone serious about making an impact.'
— **James Taylor**, keynote speaker on creativity, innovation and artificial intelligence

'*The Bookability Formula*, like Maria herself, is profoundly insightful, hilariously funny and brutally honest. It's an indispensable guide that speakers of all levels should re-read yearly to diagnose blind spots in their content and their business. (Although, if you're like me, you'll risk concussion from the number of times you'll smack your forehead thinking, "How did I miss that?")'

— **Beth Sherman**, seven-times Emmy-winning comedy writer, comedian, and speaker on using humour to connect and engage

To Adam

To your continued success

Maria x

The Bookability Formula

What the **1% most-booked speakers** do (and you can too)

MARIA FRANZONI

Re think

First published in Great Britain in 2025
by Rethink Press (www.rethinkpress.com)

© Copyright Maria Franzoni

All rights reserved. No part of this publication may be reproduced, stored in or introduced into a retrieval system, or transmitted, in any form, or by any means (electronic, mechanical, photocopying, recording or otherwise) without the prior written permission of the publisher.

The right of Maria Franzoni to be identified as the author of this work has been asserted by her in accordance with the Copyright, Designs and Patents Act 1988.

This book is sold subject to the condition that it shall not, by way of trade or otherwise, be lent, resold, hired out, or otherwise circulated without the publisher's prior consent in any form of binding or cover other than that in which it is published and without a similar condition including this condition being imposed on the subsequent purchaser.

Cover image © Adobe Stock | Vitaliy

I'd like to start by thanking you for picking up this book. It has reached your hands because of the support and encouragement of others. It has been a labour, if not so much a labour of love but more like a terrible pregnancy: there have been nausea, odd food cravings and disrupted sleep. This is the nearest I will get to giving birth. I hope it will help you give birth to new ideas and ways of working; for some of you it may birth a new career as a paid speaker.

Staying on the subject of giving birth, I would not be here, and therefore neither would this book had it not been for my wonderful parents to whom this is dedicated. They raised me with a strong work ethic, a desire to be financially independent and the belief that you can always make a good living if you keep learning. Thank you both.

And so, this book is dedicated to my parents, Lili and Giuseppe (Joe)

(And don't worry, Mum and Dad, I'm not expecting you to read it.)

Contents

Foreword	1
Introduction	3
1 Relevant (R)	13
2 Known (K) – What For And Who By	33
3 Known (K) – How To Get Known	55
4 Memorable (M)	73
5 Easy (E) – Easy To Book	93
6 Easy (E) – Easy To Work With	105
7 Value (V)	125
8 Ego (e)	143
Conclusion	165
Recommended Reading	171
Acknowledgements	175
The Author	179

Foreword

'Snappy', 'short-tempered', and 'snarling' are the words to come to mind when I think about my first encounter with Maria. You see, it was Keaton, her Coton de Tulear – trusty companion, life-long protector, and loyal canine friend – who popped round the door first. Once I'd navigated the gatekeeper (by stepping over him, he's tiny), I found Maria to be the opposite – friendly, engaging and personable, but even with her many positive qualities, the meeting was a disaster.

I'd just started my speaking career and had become busy quickly. I needed representation and wanted to capitalise on my early success. Maria told me she wasn't interested and sent me packing – in a friendly, engaging and personable way. I can't remember the reasons why, but I do remember three things that

I thought about as I peeled the parking ticket off my car in the rain. Firstly, Maria made sense and really knew her stuff; secondly, she told it how it was and her thoughts were not sugar-coated; and thirdly, bring some dog treats if I ever wanted to go back.

Time passed and I won't bother you with how eventually we decided to work together, but we did. My speaking career and business went from doing OK to being a seven-figure business quicker than you can say, 'You're on mute.'

Quite simply, Maria is the most respected sage in the business; to call her anything less would be inaccurate. I realised this during our first meeting and she proved it solidly at our next. More specifically, her advice and guidance on how to work with a bureau, how to understand a brief and work with clients, and how to construct great content were invaluable accelerants to my career. Generous with her knowledge and incisive with her judgement, it was with Maria at my side that I was able to navigate the opportunities and pitfalls that the world of paid speaking offers.

With my speaking business, Maria has become its trusty companion, life-long protector and loyal friend. I am very lucky. I hope you will be, too.

Thank you, Santa Maria, Patron Saint of speakers

Jamil Qureshi, TEDx speaker, performance coach, facilitator, entrepreneur and author

Introduction

If you're reading this book, it's likely that you have some experience or expertise that you'd like to share on stage. Perhaps you've achieved success in business, academia, or adventure. Maybe you've overcome major adversity or developed innovative solutions to big problems. Whatever your background, you have insights that others could benefit from hearing, but having expertise doesn't automatically make you bookable as a speaker. I've seen many brilliant individuals fail to turn their knowledge into a profitable speaking career. They may be passionate about their subject and have great stories to tell, but they're missing a crucial element – 'bookability', the ability to get booked.

This book is aimed at speakers who help organisations solve problems, provide solutions, and drive better outcomes. The content can be applied more broadly and to other types of speakers, but my primary focus is on those speaking at business/professional meetings, conferences, and events. It isn't a book about public speaking, which is generally unpaid, or for speakers who sell from stage. It is about paid professional speaking – speakers who get booked and paid to speak.

I'm not here to teach you how to speak; there are plenty of resources and brilliant coaches out there who are far better qualified than me for that. One of those coaches is Mary Tillson-Wharton, who I will reference regularly. Mary's expertise is in helping speakers develop their content strategy structuring and refining speeches, workshops and training programmes.

I'm going to focus on how to make yourself [more] bookable and charge higher fees for your expertise. Whether you're just starting out or looking to grow, the strategies and tactics in this book will help you accelerate that journey.

Why should you believe me?

You might be wondering, 'Why should I listen to you, Maria?' That's a good question, I'm glad you asked. I have a bit of relevant experience: I've been in the industry since 1998. For twenty-three of those years, I worked in or ran international speaker bureaus, including helping London Speaker Bureau (LSB)

INTRODUCTION

grow from being UK-only to having twenty-five offices in eighteen countries. From 2007 to 2021 I ran my own international speaker bureau while maintaining a role as 'elder and advisor' with LSB. I now work directly with speakers, teaching them the strategies and techniques used by bureaus to create profitable speaking businesses.

I should take a moment here to explain what a speaker bureau is. Simply put, a speaker bureau is a carefully curated roster of hundreds, if not thousands, of speakers covering a variety of topics, locations, languages, and fee ranges. A bureau serves as an intermediary between the booker (usually someone running a conference or event) and the speaker. The bureau agent's role is to know their roster well enough to be able to match the right speaker to a client's needs. The bureau's client is the booker – the person paying the bill; the speakers are their 'products'. Each bureau has its own vetting process to decide whether to take a speaker on, and a major consideration when making that decision is ultimately whether that speaker is likely to be bookable, in other words, can they sell them?

In my bureau career, I booked thousands of speakers for events across the world, working with a wide range of nationalities and languages on both the speaker and the client side. In fact, I worked extensively with individuals from across all continents except Australia, where the time difference meant

I felt I couldn't give clients my best. My job has been to understand my clients' needs – their event objectives and their budgets – and then match them with the right speaker. Bureaus get paid on commission once a booking is made, so bookability (or future bookability) is right at the top of the list when it comes to deciding which speakers to work with.

My years in the industry have given me a unique perspective. I know what makes a speaker bookable because I've spent years asking myself that very question every time I considered taking on someone new. It's through this lens – the booker's lens – that I'll be sharing my insights with you.

The problem with most speaking advice

There's a lot of advice out there for speakers and most of it is well intentioned. Unfortunately, it often comes from people who don't understand the speaking industry. I've had to unravel many messes where speakers have gone to video, website or branding experts who have given speakers poor advice that has resulted in few or no bookings.

There are also many speakers out there sharing their experience of how they built their businesses. Not all are what they seem. The genuine coaches are those that can show their track record of bookings and revenue. These are the people worth listening to.

INTRODUCTION

One piece of advice I hear regularly that always makes me cringe is when speakers are advised 'to start with their passion'. While this sounds nice, it's often a recipe for failure in this industry. Nobody cares about your story or your passion until they understand how it can help *them*. Clients aren't booking you for your benefit; they're booking you for their audience – to solve a problem or achieve an objective. Your passion has to relate to a problem in the marketplace, a problem that people are willing to pay you to help them solve.

Most speaker trainers know what worked for them and their topic, but with my bureau background, I know what works *regardless* of your topic, background, or industry. I've seen what gets speakers booked and what doesn't across all kinds of markets. The difference between a nice-sounding idea and a commercially successful speaking business is huge, and getting it right is what separates those who struggle from those who thrive.

The Bookability Formula

I have spent a lot of my career considering the question of 'bookability' and what it is that makes some people more frequently booked than others. Let me take you back to 2019, a record-breaking year for LSB. That year, I had a bit of an 'aha' moment that changed how I think about speaker success. I was reading Richard Koch's book, *The 80/20 Principle: The secret of achieving more with less,* and wondered if it applied to speaker bookings.

I'm sure you are familiar with the Pareto Principle (also known as the 80/20 rule) which states that 80% of results come from 20% of efforts. In his book, Richard goes further. He says that if you again apply the 80/20 rule to that top 20%, you'll find that an even smaller proportion, just 4% of that initial 20%, is responsible for more than half of the results (64%). If you take it one step further still, 20% of that 4% is once more disproportionately responsible for results, and so the pattern continues.

I wondered if this was true in the case of LSB and when I analysed booking data, I was excited to see that it was. At that time, LSB had 4,489 speakers on their roster. Of those, 836 were booked at least once that year – just under 20% of the total (18.6% to be exact). Applying the 80/20 principle again to that 836, you'd expect around 20% of the speakers (167) to be booked multiple times. In fact, 196 speakers were booked multiple times, which tracks closely.

If you take 20% of those 196, you'd expect around 39 speakers to be the most booked. The actual number? 45 speakers. This means that 1% of the total roster accounted for 80% of the bookings and over 50% of the revenue. This shocked me: we had nearly 4500 speakers from twenty-five offices in eighteen countries and across four continents, but just forty-five speakers – 1% – accounted for 80% of the bookings. Wow!

Initially, I thought that this might be a blip, that the results were simply for this particular year for LSB, so I studied the data for my own bureau (thirteen years' worth) and found the same pattern. I asked friendly bureau competitors if they had seen similar. It was not a blip; the 80/20 principle works.

I decided to look more closely at the top forty-five speakers with LSB. I expected the list to include a lot of famous names or celebrities but found that that was not the case. If you are not in the industry, you probably wouldn't recognise the majority of people listed, many of whom I have used as examples. This motivated me, with Mary Tillson-Wharton's help, to look deeper to understand what these top forty-five had that the others did not.

What we discovered was that LSB's top speakers excel in four key areas. This is in line with the second iteration of the Pareto rule, where we saw a 64:4 ratio. These top-performing speakers had four factors in common. They were:

- Highly relevant to the paying markets (R)
- Well known in the industry for one thing (K)
- Memorable to bookers and audiences (M)
- Easy to work with (E)

Being a lover of numbers and mathematics, I took the four keys one step further to create The Bookability Formula (B):

$$B = \frac{(R+K+M+E)^V}{e}$$

Let me break this down. Think of your success as a speaker as being shaped by four core variables – how relevant (R), known (K), memorable (M) and easy to work with (E) you are. The more of each of these qualities that you have, the more bookable you are. There are then two additional forces, value (V) and ego (e), that can amplify or sabotage that success.

Throughout this book, we'll explore each of these key variables in turn and I'll be showing you how to exploit these characteristics to maximise your bookability. I'll share examples from the 1%, but we'll also consider a broader cross-section of speakers, many of whom are well on their way to joining them. We'll also come across one or two well-known names – my friends regularly tell me that if name-dropping were a sport, I'd be a gold medallist.

By the time you finish this book, you'll have a clear understanding of what bookers are looking for and actions you can take to make yourself more appealing to high-paying clients. You'll learn how to:

- Identify the relevant markets for your expertise
- Build your visibility to become better known
- Make yourself memorable to bookers
- Be easy to find, book and work with
- Articulate and deliver exceptional value to your clients
- Stay humble as you become more and more successful

At its core, getting booked as a speaker isn't just about being great on stage; it's about treating speaking like a business and the most-booked speakers understand this. Just like any successful business, you need something people want to buy, and in speaking, that starts with bookability.

My promise to you

I promise that after reading this book, you'll have practical, actionable strategies and tactics to accelerate your speaking career. What might have taken years can be compressed into months with the right approach, but I won't sugarcoat things or give you feel-good platitudes. I'm direct. My nickname when I was a management consultant was 'the velvet hammer'. I'll hit you hard but I won't do lasting damage. My approach is waffle-free and focused on what works in the real world.

Also, a word of caution: the speaking life isn't for everyone. The time spent on stage is just a small part of what running a speaking business involves. Most of your time will be spent getting the gigs rather than delivering them. Once you build momentum, you'll likely spend a lot of time travelling, be away from home more than you'd expect, and feel the pressure of always having to deliver at a high level. It can be tiring, lonely and, at times, unpredictable, especially if you thrive on routine. That said, if the lifestyle suits you, it can be incredibly rewarding. You might stay in wonderful hotels, visit amazing places, travel business class, meet fascinating people, and continually learn from other experts at events. And of course, there's nothing quite like the adrenaline rush of holding an audience in the palm of your hand. But it's worth going in with your eyes open; it's a business first, a performance second.

Everything in this book is seen from the booker's perspective because that's what I know. This isn't about your passion or personal story. It's about what makes you valuable and bookable in the eyes of the people who decide who gets hired. At times, this might challenge how you see yourself as a speaker. It might even feel a little uncomfortable, but if you want a sustainable, well-paid speaking career, this is the fastest route.

If you are ready to get bookable, let's get started. How quickly you move from here is up to you.

$$B = \frac{(R+K+M+E)^v}{e}$$

1
Relevant (R)

'If you're not putting out relevant content in relevant places, you don't exist.'
— Gary Vaynerchuk, entrepreneur and CEO

The first key variable of The Bookability Formula is about being relevant. Without relevance, you risk becoming just another voice in the crowd. Relevance isn't about what you want to talk about; it's about what companies, conferences, and audiences need *right now*. If your content doesn't address those needs, you'll struggle to get booked.

In this chapter, we'll look at relevance through the booker's lens, what it really means in today's market, and how you can position yourself as the speaker they *need* to hire.

What makes a speaker relevant?

Bookers are looking for speakers who understand their world, who get their challenges, and can help their audience in a meaningful way.

Many speakers focus on themselves: their story, their achievements, their journey. Bookable speakers start with relevance:

- What's happening in the market right now?
- What challenges are organisations facing?
- What change needs to happen?
- How can I contribute to making it a reality?

If you ask these questions first, you'll position yourself as someone worth booking; if you don't, you risk blending into the crowd, becoming just another speaker talking about what *they* want to talk about instead of what bookers need to hear.

If you've ever watched *Shark Tank* or *Dragons' Den*, you'll have seen investors turning down entrepreneurs who haven't done their homework. If someone pitches an idea without the evidence to prove there's a real market for it, the investors walk away. They want to see that people are willing to pay for the product or service, not just that it's a good idea. Some entrepreneurs spend all their time perfecting their product without testing whether anyone needs or wants it. Others think their offering is big enough to warrant investment, but when asked for proof such as sales figures, market research, or customer demand, they come up short.

The same applies to speaking. Your expertise and your message might be valuable to you, but is it relevant? Have you tested it in the market? Have you positioned yourself around the problems that bookers need solving? Just like an investor won't back a business without a clear market, a booker won't hire a speaker who isn't addressing a pressing need.

Who are you selling to?

If you want to position yourself properly, you need to know who's buying your services and put them first.

A mistake I often see speakers make is assuming that if they just put themselves out there, the bookings will automatically follow, but bookers don't work like that. They need to feel prioritised and, more than anything, they need to feel understood. The better you show that you get what they need, the more likely they are to book you.

Sounds simple, but here's where it gets tricky: there's not just one type of buyer. You're dealing with lots of different people, each with their own priorities, so how can you possibly serve them all? Let's break it down. There are three main groups you need to understand: end clients, meeting professionals, and speaker bureaus. They all want great speakers but they each have different decision-making processes.

Whatever their job title, the people you deal with will fall into one of these categories, and the better you understand how each one thinks, the easier it becomes to get booked.

End clients

The end client (sometimes called the hosting client or sponsor) is the organisation running the event and ultimately paying all the bills. They might be putting on an annual conference, a leadership summit, or a client update. Whatever the event, they're booking a speaker for *their* people; that could be employees, members, customers, or prospects.

The end client is also the organisation with a problem that needs solving. An issue is affecting their ability to do their work and stopping them from achieving the results they want and they are looking for a speaker to help. If you are going to position yourself as a relevant speaker to end clients, you need to demonstrate your understanding of the problem they're facing and the relevance of your solution.

> **TIP**
>
> When pitching to an end client, include a testimonial from someone in their industry that highlights the results you delivered. It builds instant credibility and helps them see what's possible for them too.

Meeting professionals

These are the people who manage events on behalf of end clients. Their job titles vary: planner, event/conference organiser, producer, etc. Some organisations with lots of events have in-house teams, but more commonly these professionals are external freelancers or agencies brought in to run the show.

Their role covers everything from venues and logistics to content and, in many cases, sourcing and booking speakers. They need to deliver a speaker who meets the end client's objectives, but they also have their own priorities – they want to do a great job and get hired again. That means they need speakers who are reliable, brilliant on stage, and easy to work with. In the industry, we call these speakers 'a safe pair of hands'. Event professionals juggle multiple moving parts, and the last thing they want is a speaker who needs babysitting. If you make their life easier, you make yourself more bookable. We'll talk more about that later in the book.

> **TIP**
>
> A useful website for keeping up with what's going on in business and professional events is www.the-iceberg.org

Speaker bureaus

A speaker bureau's job is to match the right speaker to a client's brief. End clients and meeting professionals turn to bureaus for one or a number of the following reasons:

- **They don't have time** to research and negotiate with speakers themselves.
- **They want to reduce risk**; bureaus offer a safety net. If a speaker cancels last minute, the bureau will find a replacement.
- **They don't know who to book**, or if they do, they don't know how to book them, what their terms are, or whether they're even available.

Bureaus only make money when they successfully place a speaker. Their priority is speakers they can sell easily. They don't just need someone who is talented on stage, they need someone who speaks to the needs of their clients, delivers reliably for event professionals, and is easy to work with. Speed matters too: bureaus are often working to tight deadlines, so they need quick responses on availability, clear answers on fit, and confidence that you can work within the client's budget. The easier you make their job, the more likely they are to put you forward for opportunities.

Routes to being booked

With three different groups involved in booking speakers, it's important to think about *who* you're selling to. Yes, some high-paid speakers are booked directly by an end client, but many times, it's an event professional making the decision on who gets short-listed. If a speaker bureau is involved, that adds another layer: they could be working for the end client, the event professional, or both.

Knowing who you're talking to changes what you need to say. If you're speaking to an end client, focus on how you'll address their challenge. If it's an event professional, reassure them you're reliable and will deliver on the day. If you're dealing with a speaker bureau, they need to feel confident they've found the perfect fit for their client.

Whoever you're speaking to, never lose sight of the audience at the end of the process. I learned this the hard way. In my early days of speaker booking, I worked with the CEO of an organisation who was a huge fan of a particular guru. He was determined to book him, convinced he was the perfect choice. I had my doubts but I was too inexperienced at the time to push back or ask the right questions so we booked the speaker. On paper, he was impressive, but when he took the stage, it became clear he wasn't the right fit. His topic wasn't relevant to the operational staff he was speaking to and they quickly lost interest. This was a mistake I only made once.

Local or global relevance

Some speakers are happy working at a local level, but many I work with have their sights set on the international stage. They want to travel and expand their reach.

When I started working with artificial intelligence (AI) strategist Elin Hauge, she was one of the country's top speakers at home in Norway but she wanted to break into the international speaking circuit. She told me that, at home, being a great speaker was often enough to get booked. Because she was well-known, she was invited to speak on a wide range of topics, but on the international stage, things were different. To compete in the global market, she needed to sharpen her positioning and make it clear exactly what she spoke about and why it mattered.

Rather than creating different bios for different markets, she refined her positioning across the board, ensuring consistency everywhere. The result? It not only increased her international bookings but also led to more demand and higher fees at home. Through the process, she also learned an important lesson: sticking to your core expertise is crucial. Early on, she accepted a request to speak on a topic outside her main specialist field, and while she delivered, she knew it wasn't up to her usual standard. It was a lesson she took forward – staying focused on what she does best has made her a stronger, more bookable speaker.

Ricardo Cabete went through a similar transformation. In Portugal, he was already a successful speaker known for delivering high-energy, inspirational sessions on a variety of topics. When he decided to go international, he needed a clearer, more defined niche so that's when he repositioned himself as an emotional intelligence expert, blending his motivational style with a commercially relevant topic that had strong global appeal.

Both Elin and Ricardo succeeded because they recognised that what works locally doesn't always translate globally. They adapted, refined their positioning, and made it easy for international bookers to see exactly why they should be hired.

Staying relevant

It's tempting to chase trends to stay relevant, by the time something becomes a trend, *everyone* is talking about it, and you'll be competing with a flood of other speakers who had the same idea. To be a truly relevant, bookable speaker, you need to stay ahead of trends, not follow them.

Take Penny Mallory as an example. She started out as a speaker known for her groundbreaking achievement as the first (and, to this day, only) woman to compete for Ford in the World Rally Championship. In 2019, she was delivering keynotes on 'World-class thinking for world-class performance'. It was a strong topic and had served her well, but then the pandemic hit. Suddenly, the demand for performance-driven keynotes disappeared. Businesses weren't focused on pushing for world-class results, they were trying to survive. Almost overnight, Penny's diary emptied and her speaking business ground to a halt.

She realised that what businesses and individuals really needed in that moment wasn't world-class performance; it was mental toughness – the ability to handle uncertainty, pressure, and setbacks. Recognising the hugely changed global landscape and the resulting need to adapt, she scrapped years of material and rebuilt her positioning from the ground up, launching her new focus on mental toughness in the summer of 2020. It was a bold move and it paid off. In the final six months of 2020, she surpassed her entire revenue for 2019, a year that had already been one of her best. While many speakers were static, waiting for things to return to normal, Penny had the courage to start again, making herself relevant to the market as it was *now*, not as it had been before.

Great speakers are always evolving, adapting to market shifts while staying true to their core expertise. Sometimes, staying relevant requires more than a small pivot; it takes a complete reinvention, and speakers, like Penny, who are willing to do that are the ones who thrive. Other times, you don't need to reinvent yourself completely; just use your unique perspective to offer fresh insights on what matters *now*. However you do it, when the market moves, you need to move too. If you ever doubt the power of reinvention, just look at Madonna. Over four decades, she's consistently refreshed her image and stayed ahead of cultural shifts, filling stadiums and selling millions of records as a result.

That said, not every shift is worth following. Remember when everyone was talking about the Metaverse, Blockchain, and GDPR? GDPR had a big impact when first introduced but is now just standard practice. The Metaverse was hyped as the next digital revolution, yet for most businesses, it hasn't delivered. Blockchain was positioned as groundbreaking, but outside of cryptocurrency, its mainstream adoption remains limited.

If you've been in business long enough, you'll remember the Millennium Bug (Y2K). It was supposed to cause absolute chaos, with banks failing, power grids shutting down, even planes falling out of the sky as soon as the clocks turned. I booked a lot of speakers on the topic, but when the year 2000 arrived, most of the predicted disasters never materialised. Was it because of the extensive preparations, or was the panic overblown? Maybe, just maybe, it was the influence of and input from all the brilliant experts I booked which helped avoid the crisis. We'll never know.

True relevance isn't about chasing headlines; it's about understanding what will have a lasting impact. Stay ahead of the curve but don't get caught up in the noise.

> **TIP**
>
> If you're unsure of the latest trends, use LinkedIn and other online communities to explore your market, test ideas, and ask questions. You'll gain insights into your market that you can use to stay ahead of the curve.

Evergreen topics

Some topics never go out of demand. Organisations will always need speakers on leadership, communication, teamwork, performance, creativity, emotional intelligence, and change management. These are the staples of the speaking world, subjects I call *evergreen topics*, but even with these people-focused subjects that stand the test of time, you can't rely on the same old content. The core issues might stay the same, but the challenges around them are constantly shifting.

Take leadership. AI is changing how businesses operate, and leaders now need a different skill set. Communication? Hybrid working has made it harder to build strong connections. For the first time, we have a workforce where young employees are *true* digital natives. Are they feeling disconnected from traditional workplaces? Are managers overwhelmed by the pace of change?

These are all examples of how even timeless topics need to evolve. As a speaker, you should always be asking: 'How is my topic relevant right now?' That's what keeps you bookable.

An ongoing process

Relevance is something you have to keep working on. What bookers are looking for changes over time and if you don't keep up, you risk becoming yesterday's news, so how do you stay relevant?

First, keep your topic connected to what's happening now. If you speak on leadership, how is it affected by AI, hybrid working, or generational shifts? If you focus on resilience, what new pressures, economic uncertainties or rapid changes make it more important than ever?

Second, stay close to your market. If your clients subscribe to *Harvard Business Review*, you should too. If they're discussing industry shifts on LinkedIn, be part of the conversation. Go to the events they attend, read the publications they read, and most importantly, talk to them. The more you understand their world, the easier it is to stay relevant.

Motivational speaker and author of several books including *Natural Born Winners* (Arrow, 2004), Robin Sieger is a great example of this in action. He was already a successful speaker, but, in a conversation over lunch, I gave him some advice: 'Find out what the market is looking for and deliver content on that need.' Two years ago, he discovered that creativity and problem solving had become the number one hiring criteria in Fortune 500 companies. Drawing on his background as Head of Entertainment Development for the BBC, he developed a new masterclass on creative problem solving. He's now in high demand with tech companies, helping them develop exactly the skills they need.

Third, tailor your message. A corporate sales team, a leadership offsite, and an industry conference all have different concerns. The more you tailor what you say to the people in front of you, the more bookable you become.

In summary, stay ahead of the curve. Bookers don't want speakers who are just repeating last year's insights. Keep an eye on trends, engage in industry conversations, and be the person who helps businesses prepare for what's next.

Ask why

If you want to make yourself relevant to a booker, start by asking 'Why?':

- Why do they want a speaker on your topic?
- Why have they enquired about you?
- Why did they book you instead of someone else?

Most speakers assume they know the answers to these questions, but bookers often see things differently. The only way to be sure you're delivering real value is to hear it in their words.

Chris Voss, the former FBI hostage negotiator, used 'Why' questions in negotiation scenarios so that the hostage taker revealed what matters to them. 'Why?' is such a powerful question. When you ask a booker, 'Why me?', they'll tell you exactly what they see as your value. Maybe they're drawn to your expertise, your fresh perspective, or the way you deliver your content. Whatever it is, their answer gives you a powerful insight into what makes you bookable, and that's what you should focus on when positioning yourself.

The same applies after a speaking engagement. You may have asked the question at the time of enquiry, but I guarantee you'll get an even better answer after they have experienced your speech. It will tell you what resonated most, which helps you refine your messaging for future bookings.

Relevance isn't about what *you* think is important, but about what matters to those who book you. What is the fastest and most accurate way to find out what that is? Ask them.

Being relevant pays

Let me give you a couple of examples of relevance in action. The first example is a speaker who wishes to remain nameless, I don't think he wants his wife to know just yet. When he first came to me, he had been working long-term in corporate but had recently left his job. He wasn't entirely sure what was next but he wanted to investigate professional speaking. I encouraged him to set himself up as an 'expert who speaks' rather than a speaker, and to create a portfolio of services. Because of that positioning – offering solutions as well as speaking – he has been able to respond to the market by delivering what organisations and individuals need.

Fast forward a year, and he's bringing in $20K a month, offering a mixture of speaking, training, and consulting programmes. He now needs to employ people to help him. It's not all been easy. He told me that it's been a tough year, with long hours and hard work, but he's stayed focused, he's listened to the market, and he's adapted.

For the second, we're going back to the early days of the pandemic again, a brutal time for the speaking industry as events disappeared overnight. I know, not the nicest memory, but stick with me.

Jamil Qureshi, a performance coach and psychologist, was at the top of his game before lockdown. Then, like so many speakers, his diary emptied almost overnight as one booking after another was cancelled. Instead of panicking, Jamil asked himself a question: 'What do my clients need right now, and how can I help?' He realised that, in the middle of all the uncertainty, leaders didn't need a keynote speech, they needed ongoing support. Rather than selling one-off speeches, he positioned himself as a performance psychologist 'on call' to advise and support leadership teams through the crisis. Most of his clients jumped at the chance, and instead of a single speaking fee, he secured monthly retainers.

Jamil stayed relevant because he didn't cling to what he used to offer, but instead adapted to what his clients needed in the moment.

Relevant: Action points

Here are some simple, practical steps to make sure you stay relevant to bookers and audiences.

1. **Know what's keeping your market up at night.** Make a list of the top five to ten challenges your ideal clients are facing right now. Read industry news, follow conversations on LinkedIn, and ask your network directly.

2. **Connect your expertise to their problems.** For each challenge, write down how your insights can help. Be clear about the outcome – what changes for them after they hear you speak?

3. **Update how you position yourself.** Look at your website, LinkedIn and speaker bio. Do they focus on the problems you solve or are they just listing what you talk about? Shift the focus to emphasise what's in it for the booker.

4. **Keep an eye on trends.** Sign up to speaker bureau and industry newsletters to find out what they are focused on right now.

5. **Get useful feedback.** After each speech, ask what felt most relevant. What stuck? What was most useful? These answers will help you refine your positioning.

6. **Be where your clients are.** Find the events, conferences and online spaces where your

prospects gather. Show up, listen, and join the conversation, whether as a speaker, panellist, or active participant.

7. **Test what resonates.** Post about new ideas and insights on LinkedIn and notice what sparks engagement. The topics that get the most interest are likely to be the ones the market cares about most.

8. **Make it easy for bookers to see your relevance.** Showcase recent work that aligns with current challenges, case studies, testimonials, or examples of how your insights have helped organisations. Keep your marketing materials fresh so bookers can immediately see why you're the right fit.

9. **Check in regularly.** Every few months, step back and ask: 'Am I still speaking about the most important issues in my market?' If not, adjust.

10. **Talk to the right people.** Stay in touch with event planners, speaker bureaus, and past clients, not to sell, but to ask about what's happening in their industry. The more you understand their challenges, the easier it is to stay ahead.

$$B = \frac{(R + K + M + E)^v}{e}$$

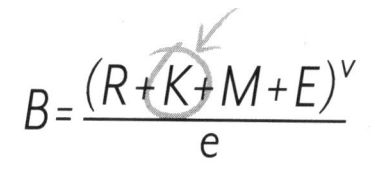

2
Known (K) – What For and Who By

> 'I've doubled down on growing my personal brand because if bookers don't know who I am they can't book me, and I can't help their delegates.'
> — Alison Edgar, motivational speaker

Once you're confident you're a relevant speaker, it's time to get yourself known. This is the **K** in The Bookability Formula. Because being known is such a fundamental element of any successful speaking career, I have divided this variable across two chapters. This first chapter concentrates on what to be known for, and who to be known by. It is concerned with developing a better understanding of what people might want and what you can offer them. It is about developing a unified, cohesive, and desirable identity as a speaker, and coming to understand your place in the market. We will explore how to ensure you are what people want and need, as well as being clear about who should know you. In the next chapter, we will move on to look at how to get known.

Being known isn't about luck, it's about strategically building a reputation so that the right people associate your name with your expertise. If no one knows who you are or what you speak about, they can't book you. When you're known in the right circles, everything gets easier: bookings come more naturally, your credibility increases, and you can charge more.

Being known isn't the same as being famous. Fame is broad recognition, often for its own sake, while being known as a speaker means you're recognised within your niche as a trusted authority. You don't need millions of followers or mainstream media attention; you just need the right people to know you exist. That means conference organisers, event planners, industry decision-makers, and potential clients who are actively looking for speakers like you.

There are two aspects to this:

1. Being known for a specific area of expertise
2. Being known by the people who book (and pay) for that expertise

Identifying your specialist subject

If you're a globally known name like Jeff Bezos or Oprah Winfrey, you can talk about whatever you like. If you've just stepped down as the CEO of a well-known brand, you might get booked based on your experience rather than a specific topic. Then there are the 'celebrities' of the speaking world – people like Brené Brown and Simon Sinek – who have earned the right to pick and choose their topic.

Until you reach that level, you'll get booked more by specialising. I get why this might feel like the wrong approach when you're starting out. You might think, 'Surely, to get known, I need to cover lots of topics, be visible everywhere, and give bookers plenty of options?'

I see it all the time: new speakers, keen to build a name and reputation, who feel they need to list every topic under the sun. You name it, they'll talk about it.

Take teamwork and personal development speaker, Paul Adamson, for example. When he first started, he positioned himself as an expert on leadership, teamwork, motivation, performance, change, resilience, and mental toughness. All great topics, but together, they lacked cohesiveness and bookers couldn't immediately establish if he was the right speaker for their event.

It wasn't until he honed his focus and defined his expertise as 'Navigating and thriving through change and adversity' that things really started to shift. That clarity made it easier for bookers to place him, bureaus to sell him, and audiences to immediately grasp his value.

This idea of starting with one clear focus isn't just true in speaking. It's how many of the world's biggest companies began. Amazon started with one product: books. Jeff Bezos didn't try to sell everything at once. He focused on dominating a single category, becoming known for it and building trust with customers, and only after that did Amazon expand into other areas like electronics, fashion, groceries, and cloud computing.

Nike followed a similar pattern, beginning with just shoes. Not clothing, not gym bags, not tech; just performance footwear. They built a reputation for innovation, quality, and credibility in that one area, which gave them permission to expand into apparel and other categories later.

It's the same principle when it comes to building your bookability. Start narrow, go deep, build trust, and then broaden your offer. Depth is more valuable than range. The more you focus on a topic, the more unique your insights become. You develop your own take, your own perspective, and that's what makes you stand out. Speakers with vague, general content get overlooked.

If you're struggling to narrow your focus, go back to the relevance chapter – the work you did there will help. It's worth taking the time, because once you're known for something specific, bookers come to you, instead of the other way around.

Staying interested so you stay interesting

Being known and staying known is about consistency. To be consistent you need to stay interested and that means picking a topic you're willing to commit to. If you chase trends or pick a topic just because it's in demand right now, but you have no real interest in it, you'll struggle to sustain the enthusiasm needed to keep talking about it. You'll be delivering your talk over and over again, refining it, expanding on it, and discussing it with bookers, audiences, and clients. If the subject doesn't hold your attention long-term, you'll get bored, and when that happens, it will show.

The most successful speakers find the sweet spot between what they love talking about, what they're great at, and what the market is willing to pay for. If one of those elements is missing, you'll struggle. A topic you love but that nobody books won't pay the bills. A high-demand topic you're not interested in will quickly feel like a chore. Choose an area where you can see yourself staying engaged for years, not months.

Before you commit to a topic, ask yourself:

- Does this topic align with my long-term goals and expertise?
- Am I excited to dive deeper into this subject and keep learning?
- Can I consistently create fresh content and insights around this topic?

Choosing the right topic isn't just about the market, it's about you, too. Pick something you can stay interested in, that plays to your strengths, and that you'll be proud to be known for in the years to come.

What is your red thread?

Once you've committed to your topic, you want to deliver a consistent message that will be instantly associated with you. If your expertise feels scattered or unfocused, it's much harder for people to remember what you stand for. This is where a red thread comes in.

A red thread is a central theme or question that runs through everything you do as a speaker. It keeps your message tight, helps you stay on track, and makes it easier for people to connect you with your area of expertise. The more consistently you apply it, the faster you become known for your topic. You'll need to be really disciplined with your message. Every way you show up – your website, your showreel, your social media, even the images you use – should reinforce that central message, the red thread.

Think about the British Olympic rowing eight at the Sydney 2000 Olympics. Their red thread was a simple but powerful question: 'Will it make the boat go faster?' Every decision they made, about training, nutrition, strategy, etc, was filtered through this question. If something didn't contribute to their goal of winning gold, they didn't do it.

Now, apply this to your speaking career. If your expertise is innovation in the workplace, your red thread might be 'Helping leaders foster a culture of innovation'; if your focus is resilience, it might be 'Helping people stay strong in high-pressure environments'. Everything you do – your talks, your content, your marketing – should reinforce this one theme. It makes decision-making easier, keeps you focused, and ensures that bookers can immediately understand what you stand for.

This might sound simple, but simple doesn't mean easy. Your red thread isn't just a tagline; it's a filter. When you apply it consistently, you become known for it. Bookers will associate you with your core message, making you more memorable, more bookable, and more in demand.

When this is done well, it becomes part of your identity as a speaker. Think of Simon Sinek – he's the 'Start with Why' guy; or Nilofer Merchant, who's known for 'Mighty Ideas'. When your message is clear and consistent, people remember you for it. James Taylor, for example, speaks on 'SuperCreativity'. He has a common name, so internet searches by name are unlikely to be immediately successful. Instead of people searching for *James Taylor* after seeing him speak, they search for 'SuperCreativity' because that's the idea he's become known for.

When your concept is strong enough, people remember *that* first and it leads them straight back to you. See if you can identify the red thread - the central idea or question that will help you stand out and become known. Find it, use it, and let it shape everything you do.

Getting known

Being known isn't just about visibility, it's also about being known by the right people. In the speaking world, that means event organisers, corporate decision-makers, and conference managers – the ones who control budgets, plan events, and select speakers. Key to remember is that they're not booking for themselves, they're booking for their audiences, and if they don't see a clear fit, they won't book you. When the right bookers know who you are and understand exactly who you serve, opportunities come more easily, often leading to multiple bookings from the same organisation.

Just as you can't speak about everything, you also can't market yourself to everyone, not if you want to get booked. Many speakers assume their message applies broadly so they try to appeal to everyone, but bookers are looking for the right speaker for their specific audience. The clearer you are about who you serve, the easier it is for bookers to see you as the right fit, making you far more bookable.

I saw this when I was working in speaker bureaus. When we met with potential new speakers, the first question we asked was, 'Who is your ideal audience?' If they couldn't answer clearly, we knew we'd struggle to book them. Bookers need to know exactly who a speaker is for so they can make the perfect match.

I'll use myself as an example. I speak on growing a speaking business, a topic that, in theory, could apply to any business. The principles I teach work just as well for SMEs, solopreneurs, and even corporate professionals looking to raise their profile. Could I therefore speak at a business growth conference? Yes. Could I talk to entrepreneurs looking to scale their businesses? Absolutely… but I don't. I only speak to speakers, specifically speakers who want to get paid to speak. Not just any speakers, but those who are serious about turning their expertise into income. That's who I tailor everything to and who I want to be known by. I have identified my ideal audience and everything I do is focused on and targeted towards maintaining this red thread of consistency and relevance.

Here's another example from round-the-world yachtsman Brendan Hall: 'I speak to organisations who have leaders and teams that are seemingly pulling in different directions. Their people are committed to the vision, and understand their own part of it, but struggle to work together as a single unit to achieve it.' To get booked, Brendan needs to be known by HR directors, L&D managers, and senior leaders responsible for leadership development and team alignment. He has worked hard to build both his profile and his relevance and is in constant demand as a result.

The clearer you are, the easier it is to get booked

When you are clear on who needs to know you, everything becomes easier. Marketing yourself is simpler because you know exactly who you are and who you're speaking to, and bookers can immediately see if you're the right fit, there's no confusion. Your message lands more effectively because it's designed for the people who need to hear it.

Take a speaker on leadership, for example. Leadership is broad. Are you speaking to corporate leaders, small business owners, first-time managers, or senior executives? The challenges each group faces are different. A first-time manager isn't thinking about global strategy, and a CEO isn't struggling with how to delegate for the first time.

At this point, I can hear you saying, 'But Maria, I want to speak to all of these groups. I want to help as many people as possible.' I get it, but think of it as a sequencing issue rather than a restriction. It's not a 'no', it's a 'not yet'. The smartest approach is to dominate one space first. Spend your first few years establishing yourself as the go-to speaker for a specific industry or sector, maybe it's the C-suite, or consultancies, or tech startups. Once you've built a strong reputation in that space, you can expand into others.

The most-booked speakers are strategic about the highest and best use of their content. They don't try to appeal to everyone at once; they build credibility, demand, and a track record in one area before moving to another. This isn't about limiting your impact – it's about maximising it. The more specific you are about who you serve, the easier it is to position yourself as the go-to speaker in your topic. Ask yourself:

- Who benefits most from what I speak about?
- Who is already looking for this kind of insight?
- Who has the budget to pay for it?
- Who do I want to work with?

Once you're clear on this, stick to it. A niche doesn't limit you; it makes you more bookable. Just like I don't try to speak to every business owner out there, you don't have to appeal to everyone either. The goal isn't to be available to everyone, it's to be known by the right people.

Growing relationships

Most organisations don't just run one event. They have a mix of internal and external events, large conferences for clients and prospects, internal leadership meetings, and smaller, more focused team sessions. Many speakers focus on getting booked *once*, but there's far more potential than that. Once you are known and trusted, there's scope for repeat bookings across multiple events.

Think about Apple's product suite. Once you buy an iPhone, Apple doesn't just stop there. They want you to invest in an iPad, a MacBook, AirPods, and so on. It's a seamless ecosystem designed to keep you engaged with their brand. Speakers can take a similar approach by offering different levels of value at different price points. Your £10K keynote might be the entry point, but what about a £100 resource, a £5K workshop, or a £100K consulting package? By creating a range of offerings, you give bookers multiple ways to work with you, increasing the lifetime value of each client.

Go deep and a little wide. Deep, by becoming indispensable to your clients so they book you repeatedly across different events, and wide, by offering solutions beyond just a speech, workshops, training, books, consulting, and digital content that continue to deliver value long after you've left the stage. The most bookable speakers don't just think about the next booking; they think about the bigger picture.

The first step to finding the right bookers is identifying the industries and sectors that align with your expertise. If you speak on 'Leadership through change', for example, industries like technology, finance, and healthcare, where transformation is constant, are natural fits. If your topic is resilience, you might look at sectors with high-pressure environments like law, emergency services, and elite sports. If you are unsure where your expertise is best placed, it is easy to find out by looking at other speakers who cover your topic and seeing which industries they speak to most.

Next, find out who is in charge of booking speakers, because it's not always obvious, and unlike in speaker bureaus or agencies where everyone is involved in booking speakers, in other organisations it could be anyone. The person responsible could be a PA, a CEO, an intern, or a VP of Communications. When I worked in speaker bureaus, we just asked, 'Who organises your conferences and events?' It's a simple question but it gets you straight to the people who make booking decisions.

Once you know the right people, build relationships with them. Connect on LinkedIn, attend industry events, and engage with their content. Don't wait for them to find you; reach out with tailored introductions that show how your talk solves a problem they're facing.

By focusing on the right bookers, those who actively need speakers in your topic, you'll build a stronger, more targeted reputation. The goal isn't just to get booked once, but to become the speaker they turn to again and again. You want this to be a long-term relationship because you are a problem solver and not a speaker.

Financial Advisor and speaker Gavin Ingham asked a client who had booked him over a dozen times why they kept booking him, and other speakers only once or twice. They said that, obviously, he did a great job, but second, and perhaps more importantly, that he was the only person who really kept in touch and showed any real interest in them and their world when there wasn't a gig in the offing. The relationship felt authentic and personal, and this mattered.

Speaker bureaus: When (and when not) to approach them

Many speakers assume that getting listed with a bureau is the key to a successful career. It's not. Bureaus are great once you're established but approaching them too early can do more harm than good. If they turn you down, they'll remember that they rejected you but they won't necessarily remember why. I've seen this happen time and time again. In fact, I've done it myself – I've passed on speakers who later became hugely successful simply because they weren't quite ready when they first approached me.

Speaker bureaus work on commission. Their priority is to sell speakers who are already in demand, not to develop new talent. Unless you have a strong existing profile, meaning you're getting booked regularly and paid well, it's unlikely they'll take you on. Worse, if they do list you before you're established, they may position you as a low-fee speaker and that label can be difficult to shift.

How, then, do you get to the point where bureaus want to work with you? You focus first on doing the work.

1. **Build your market presence.** Before bureaus will take you seriously, you need to build your market presence. There are a number of things you need to ensure you have done first:

- **Be clear on what you speak about:** If you don't know exactly what you offer, bookers won't either.

- **Get paid to speak:** If you're only speaking for free, you're not ready for a bureau.

- **Have a professional presence:** Your website, bio, and showreel should reflect the level of speaker they can confidently put in front of their clients.

- **Generate demand:** If bookers aren't already coming to you, bureaus won't be interested either.

2. **Establish credibility.** Bureaus typically look for speakers who are consistently booking engagements in the 5—10K range or higher. If you're not yet there, focus on:

- **Raising your fees:** You need to be comfortable quoting a commercial rate that reflects your expertise.

- **Building repeat business:** When clients book you again, it shows you're delivering real value.

- **Increasing visibility:** Be active in your industry, share your expertise, and position yourself as a speaker worth knowing.

3. **Approach bureaus in the right way.** Once you're speaking regularly at a commercial rate, you can start approaching bureaus strategically:

- **Make it easy for them:** Tailor your approach, and follow the instructions they provide on their websites about applying to them.

- **Start with the right bureaus:** Bureaus have different client basis and specialities so make sure that you are approaching a bureau that is a good match for you.

- **Leverage introductions:** A warm referral from a happy client carries a lot of weight.

Bureaus are a valuable route to market if you're the right fit, but they won't build your business for you. They want speakers who are already known, booked, and easy to sell. The stronger your profile, the more interest you'll get from them, rather than the other way around.

Of course, there are exceptions. If you've done something extraordinary or have a topical, high-profile story, bureaus may come knocking. When astronaut Tim Peake returned from space, bureaus wanted him immediately; Nick Leeson was booked heavily after the collapse of Barings Bank; former heads of state and political figures are instantly bookable – think of Condoleezza Rice or Barack Obama; and when Hollywood tells your story, the demand skyrockets. Frank Abagnale (from *Catch Me If You Can*), Chris Gardner (*The Pursuit of Happyness*), and Erin Brockovich all became highly sought-after speakers after their stories hit the big screen, but let's be honest, we're probably not going to have a blockbuster film made about our lives.

> **TIP**
>
> If you want to see if you are 'speaker bureau ready', go to www.mariafranzoni.me/bookability for my Speaker Bureau Ready checklist.

Industry events and associations

Every sector has trade associations and professional membership organisations and most run at least one major annual conference. Many also organise smaller events, exhibitions, networking sessions, and specialist forums throughout the year, and most of them involve speakers in some capacity.

The demand for business events is enormous. According to a 2023 report by the Events Industry Council and Oxford Economics, the global business events industry in 2019 contributed $2.8 trillion in total economic impact and supported 10.9 million jobs worldwide. Within that, direct spending on events amounted to $1.15 trillion, with a $662.6 billion contribution to global GDP.[1]

---

1. Events Industry Council and Oxford Economics, *2023 Global Economic Significance of Business Events* (Events Industry Council, 2023), www.iaee.com/wp-content/uploads/2023/10/EIC-ESS-Executive-Summary.pdf, accessed 7 April 2025

Associations can be a great route into the speaking market. If your ideal booker is in HR, there are HR associations, and if you want to speak to professional meeting planners, organisations like MPI (Meeting Professionals International) are full of them. There are even associations for speaker bureaus and talent agencies. Some associations pay well for speakers, particularly at their flagship events, while others may have little or no budget, but even when the fee isn't high, these events can be valuable in other ways. Associations are full of decision-makers and if you become a trusted speaker within their network, more opportunities tend to follow. Many organisations don't just run events for their members; they also hold internal conferences for employees, client events, and leadership retreats. If you establish yourself as a valuable expert and go-to resource, there's plenty of scope for repeat work.

> **TIP**
>
> If an association doesn't have a budget for speakers, ask if they'll give you a membership instead. That gives you direct access to their members which can be a great way to connect with potential bookers.

People will talk

'The more you speak, the more you speak' is a phrase you may well have heard. Essentially, it means that work leads to more work, but only if you're good. If you deliver a great speech, people will talk about you, recommend you, and book you.

Motivational speaker Brad Burton says that his business grows because people talk about him. He does a great job on stage, and that leads to referrals. His strategy?

- Be so good that people can't ignore you.
- Be memorable enough that people talk about you.
- Be different enough that people remember you.

That all sounds ever so simple, but surely the key question is then, how do you get good? There are several easy steps you can take that may help.

The first is to start small. Get plenty of experience in delivering shorter sessions, participating in panel discussions, and testing your content in lower-pressure environments. Practise in safe spaces: speaking associations, networking groups, and local meetups are great places to refine your material before taking it to paying clients.

The next step is to take yourself online. Use social media and podcasts and test important points from your talk as posts, videos, or podcast interviews to see what resonates. Watch yourself back: record your talks and analyse what works, and what doesn't so you can improve, but also ask for real feedback from those present. Ask trusted peers and audience members for honest input. You can also employ an expert, or work with a speech or presentation expert such as Mary Tillson-Wharton.

Your speech is never 'finished', and there's always room to improve, but at some point, you've got to take the plunge. Put yourself out there, get the experience, and keep refining as you go.

The next chapter addresses perhaps the most important part of being known, and that is how to market yourself successfully.

Known – What for and who by: Action points

Here are ten action points to help you develop what you want to be known for and who you want to be known by:

1. **Define your niche.** The more specific your expertise, the more bookable you become. Avoid being a generalist.
2. **Find your red thread.** Identify a central theme or question that runs through all your work, like, 'Will it make the boat go faster?'
3. **Choose a topic that sustains your interest.** Don't follow trends. Select something you're passionate about and can speak on for years.

4. **Align your expertise with your long-term goals.** Make sure your speaking topic reflects what you want to be known for over time.

5. **Test your positioning.** Refine your focus by identifying what the market responds to and what bookers want.

6. **Ensure your topic fits both your strengths and market demand.** Use a Venn diagram of what you love, what you're good at and what people will pay for.

7. **Be consistent with your message.** Apply your red thread to your website, bio, social content and showreel so it all reinforces your core idea.

8. **Decide who your ideal audience is.** Clarity here helps you tailor your message and be easier to place.

9. **Assess your readiness to build a personal brand.** Being known starts with being clear about what you want to be known for.

10. **Commit to mastery before expansion.** Focus on becoming the go-to speaker in one niche before trying to speak to broader audiences.

$$B = \frac{(R+K+M+E)^v}{e}$$

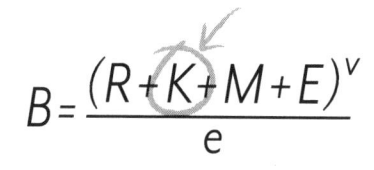

3
Known (K) – How To Get Known

'The best-known beats the best.'
— John Lee, entrepreneur and investor

In this second half of the consideration of being known, we shall look at how to market yourself successfully and how to increase your chances of being seen by the right people at the right time. This means making the most of the technology that positions you directly in front of those who matter, but also remembering that speaking is a human-to-human business, and that being known means making and maintaining successful relationships.

Marketing yourself

If no one knows who you are, they can't book you. It's as simple as that, but it's also where many speakers struggle. Getting known requires sales and marketing, and most speakers don't like promoting themselves. I see this resistance all the time. I even had a sales speaker tell me he wasn't good at selling himself (yes, really). If you can't sell yourself and yet your expertise is sales, maybe rethink your career? I didn't take him on.

I do get it – selling yourself can feel awkward. The good news is you don't have to. Instead of focusing on selling *you*, shift the focus to selling your speech, your expertise, and the outcomes you deliver. When a client books you, they aren't hiring you just because you're a nice person. They're hiring you because they believe you'll make an impact, so talk about that.

Taking your speaking career seriously means taking control of your visibility. That means marketing yourself. There's no way around it, and no, you can't outsource all of it. You can get help with some tasks, but ultimately, no one else will care about your career as much as you do.

Marketing doesn't mean plastering your name everywhere. It means making sure the right people – those who book speakers – know what you do and why they should care. That means maintaining three key characteristics in anything and everything people see about you. These are:

1. **Consistency:** If bookers see your name, website, or social media, it should be clear who you are and what you speak about.
2. **Relevance:** Your message should reflect what's going on in your industry and what clients are looking for.
3. **Repetition:** It takes multiple touchpoints before someone decides to book you. You must be visible.

When I first started in speaker bureaus, I spent three hours a day making phone calls and sending faxes. (Yes, I was around for faxes; I've even worked with telexes, I'm that old.) Now we have LinkedIn, emails, social media, WhatsApp, video messages, and more. There's no excuse for not staying in touch with your market.

The downside? The modern world is noisy. You won't get booked just because you posted on LinkedIn once or sent an email. Studies suggest it takes 7–13 touchpoints before someone makes a buying decision.[2] You might not even realise someone is following your work until they suddenly say, 'I've been watching

---

2   P Harsh, 'How Many Touchpoints Before a Sale? Revealing the Magic Number for Success', alore (25 June 2024), www.alore.io/blog/how-many-touchpoints-before-a-sale, accessed 4 April 2025

your posts all year,' so mix it up and try different approaches. You won't always know which one will work, but you have to keep going.

However advanced the world becomes, human interactions will always remain at the core, and key to a successful speaking business is ensuring that those interactions are positive. This business runs on building successful relationships. You can automate some tasks but nothing replaces genuine relationships. I've lost count of how many times I've received an email that starts with 'Dear (First Name)' because someone rushed an automated campaign.

Building relationships takes patience but it pays off. The biggest deal of my career? It took ten years. I spent a decade staying in touch with an event professional in Miami. We had friendly chats, shared industry news, and stayed connected, without a single booking. Then, in 2019, he gave me the biggest contract of my career, worth a cool million dollars. I wish that was the end of the story, but the events were scheduled for 2020. You can guess what happened next…

Using social media to get booked

Right now, LinkedIn is the best social media platform for speakers. It's where you'll find end clients, event professionals, and speaker bureaus. Even if they don't post much, many are watching, keeping an eye on trends and potential speakers. It's not the only platform though, and, depending on your topic, others might work too. I know speakers who have built strong followings on Instagram, X, and TikTok.

YouTube, however, deserves special attention. Unlike other platforms, it focuses solely on video – exactly what bookers want to see. If you don't have a YouTube channel, you're missing an opportunity to showcase your speaking style. A well-edited reel or even short clips of you in action can make all the difference in getting booked. Plus, since YouTube is owned by Google, videos tend to rank well in search results, though with AI reshaping searches, this may change.

When it comes to social media strategy, I take inspiration from Gary Vaynerchuk (Gary Vee). He built his brand by turning his father's liquor store into a multimillion-dollar business through a simple concept: giving value upfront. His YouTube series, *Wine Library TV*, wasn't a sales pitch; it was free, engaging content that made wine accessible to everyday people. That approach made him a trusted voice and his business grew as a result.

His advice for social media? 'Give value, give value, give value, and then ask for business.' For some speakers, that sounds counterintuitive – why give away your best ideas? – but in doing so, you remove any doubt about your expertise. Bookers start to know, like, and trust you, and if the free stuff is *that* good, they'll assume that what you actually charge for must be worth every penny.

I've experienced this myself. I've purchased all of solopreneur and influencer Justin Welsh's products just from following him on LinkedIn. I've never spoken to him or even met him yet I trust him completely. His content is so consistently valuable that I've not only bought from him but I also tell others to do the same. That's the power of using social media well: he's never had to sell to me directly because his posts did all the work.

Social media is a speaker's best tool for staying visible and building credibility with the right people. Done well, it helps you establish relationships before you've even met someone in person. Whether it's posting insights, joining discussions, or sharing valuable content, the more useful you are, the more bookers will notice you.

My advice? Don't treat social media as a sales platform, treat it as a relationship-building tool. Show up, share value, and watch what happens.

> **TIP**
>
> Be consistent. Use the same photo, strapline, and messaging across all your contact points – your website, social media, emails, and so on. Bookers need to recognise it's you.

Using LinkedIn to get known

LinkedIn is one of the platforms where more and more event organisers, speaker bureaus, and corporate decision-makers research and shortlist speakers. If you're not using it well, you're missing opportunities.

Here's a quick guide on what I've seen works:

- **Show up daily:** Engage with posts, comment thoughtfully, and stay visible.

- **Write for the lurkers:** Most bookers won't engage but they're watching. Stay consistent.

- **Give value, not just updates:** Share insights, lessons, and industry trends.

- **Optimise your profile:** Your headline should highlight the problem you solve, not just your title.

- **Create a content system:** Break down your keynotes, repurpose content, and use audience questions as post ideas.

- **Sell without selling:** Show expertise consistently so bookers come to you when they need a speaker.

- **Personalise your outreach:** Avoid cold pitches. Start real conversations and build relationships.

Play the long game, stay visible, add value, and let LinkedIn do the work for you.

Getting known through traditional media

Traditional media still has its place in the speaking industry. Being featured in an industry magazine, website, or even a national newspaper gives you third-party validation and reinforces your credibility as an expert. Many speakers start this way, writing articles or being quoted in publications relevant to their field.

TV and radio are much harder to crack but not impossible. If you have a compelling story, strong opinions on a topical issue, or unique expertise, media outlets may be interested, but don't wait for them to find you, proactively pitch yourself when relevant opportunities arise.

Some speakers actively use media to build their profile and make themselves the go-to expert in their field. Captain Emma Henderson MBE, former airline pilot, author, and speaker, is a great example. She first became known through the ITV documentary *Inside the Cockpit* (2019), which gave her visibility and valuable media training. She then leveraged that recognition when she co-founded Project Wingman, a charity supporting NHS staff by setting up 'first-class lounges' in hospitals during the COVID-19 pandemic, providing them with a space to decompress and recharge. This led to extensive press coverage, interviews, and even a meeting with the Prime Minister. When she was awarded an MBE, she ensured her story was well-publicised, reinforcing her credibility further.

Because Emma was already a known quantity and a safe pair of hands for journalists, the media kept coming back. Over time, she built strong relationships with journalists, always making herself easy to find, quick to respond, and ready with clear, concise answers. As a result, when aviation stories hit the news, such as the Singapore turbulence incident (May 2024) or the mid-air collision between a plane and a helicopter over Washington (January 2025), she was the one broadcasters called.

Guesting on podcasts

Not all speakers will get the same opportunities as Emma, but a route that is accessible to all is guesting on podcasts. Podcasts allow you to showcase your expertise, reach new audiences, and refine your ability to deliver clear, engaging answers. Many industries now have well-established podcasts, and hosts are often looking for knowledgeable guests. While it's tempting to aim for the biggest names straight away, start by saying yes to as many relevant opportunities as possible. The more you practise, the better you'll get.

I've interviewed many speakers and the ones who stand out are those who can answer a question in a well-structured, succinct way, without launching into a full-scale monologue. That takes practice. Since launching my own podcast, I know I've improved simply by doing it repeatedly.

Some speakers don't stop there, and create their own podcasts to position themselves in their niche. James Taylor wanted to establish himself in the creativity space, so he launched a podcast where he interviewed other speakers and experts in the field. This meant that whenever someone searched for those well-known names, his name appeared alongside. As his interviews gained traction, he was able to attract even bigger guests, raising his profile yet further.

Hosting a podcast is a commitment, but it has real benefits: it builds authority, strengthens your network, and creates content you can repurpose across multiple platforms. Whether you're appearing as a guest or running your own show, podcasts are a powerful tool to establish yourself and stay visible.

So, whether it's an industry publication, a podcast, or a media appearance, think of interviews as another tool in your speaking toolkit. The ability to communicate your expertise concisely and confidently isn't just useful for media, it makes you a better speaker overall.

Your website and showreel: The digital shop window

If you're serious about being known as a speaker, you need a website. It doesn't have to be fancy, expensive, or complex, but it does need to look professional and clearly position you as a speaker. Imagine a booker finds you on LinkedIn or hears about you from someone else. The next thing they'll do? Google you. If they can't find a website, or worse, they find a weak, outdated one, you risk losing the booking before you've even had a conversation.

Your website is your digital shop window. It should instantly answer these questions for bookers:

- **Who are you?** Outline your expertise, credibility, and authority.

- **Who do you help?** What sort of challenges are they facing?

- **What do you speak about?** What are your specialist subjects and topics?

- **Why should they book you?** What results and impact will you bring?

- **What should they do next?** Make it easy for them: should they book a call, check your availability, fill out a form, or contact you directly?

Your speaker website

A strong speaker website should contain the following:

- **A clear, compelling homepage.** Within five seconds, a booker should know what you speak about and why you're worth booking. Avoid generic 'Welcome to my website' intros, and be clear, bold, and to the point.

- **A strong speaker bio.** Not a dry CV or a long-winded life story, this should focus on your expertise, your credibility, and the impact you have. Make sure it's written with bookers in mind and doesn't just list your career highlights.

- **Professional photos and branding.** Invest in high-quality images – bookers want to see what you look like on stage. If your branding (colours, fonts, style) is consistent, you'll be more recognisable across all platforms.

- **Your showreel or video clips.** If you have a professional showreel, great; make it easy to find. If you don't, at least have a simple, well-lit video of you speaking to the camera or delivering a talk. Make it booker-friendly: no long intros and no fancy effects, just you speaking, engaging, and delivering value.

- **Topics and takeaways.** Bookers need to know what they're booking at a glance. Have a section clearly outlining your speaking topics.

- **Testimonials and social proof.** Bookers trust other bookers so include testimonials, client logos, case studies, or media features. If you've worked with recognisable brands, industries, or events, highlight them.
- **Easy-to-find contact details.** You'd be amazed how many speakers hide their contact details behind forms. Make it easy for bookers to reach you with a clear 'Book Me' or 'Contact' page, with an email address, phone number, and social media links.

Showreels

Now let's talk about showreels, also known as demo reels or speaker reels.

When I first started giving the sort of advice that led to this book, I assumed speakers would be most interested in topics like understanding the market, positioning themselves, setting their fees, and finding bookers. While these are all crucial, the number one question I get asked is, 'How do I create a great showreel?'

A good showreel is certainly an important tool, but it shouldn't come first. Before you invest in a professional showreel, you need to be clear on your target audience, your expertise, and your speaking topics. If you don't know exactly how you want to position yourself, a showreel won't help; in fact, it'll just be a well-produced piece of confusion. Make sure you've laid the foundations before you lay anything down on film.

A booker does need to see some video before hiring you, but don't rush into creating a professional reel. If you're just getting started, a simple video to camera can be enough. Record yourself speaking directly to bookers, explaining what you do and why your message matters. This will give them an insight into your speaking style while you test the market and refine your positioning.

> **TIP**
>
> I can hear you shouting at me that you want more on showreels. Go to www.mariafranzoni.me/bookability and you'll find my guide to making a showreel that will get you booked.

When the time is right, a good showreel is one of your most valuable marketing assets, alongside a strong website and, of course, a great speech. Your website makes you easy to find, your showreel makes you easy to trust, and your speech makes you easy to book again. If you don't have a website yet, start there, and if you're stressing about your showreel, make sure you've got clarity before you worry about production quality. When you're ready, both will work together to help you get known, get booked, and build momentum.

Getting known takes time

Getting known doesn't happen overnight. It takes time, effort, and consistent repetition. Even once you're regularly booked, you still need to sell and market your speeches and services. US Customer Experience speaker David Avrin rightly says that, 'Speaking isn't a business. Getting the gig is the business. Speaking is the performance – the part we all love. Like any business, sales and marketing brings the opportunities and revenue.' I tell speakers wanting to get into the industry that 80% of the speaking business is getting the business, so my question to you is are you spending 80% of your time on sales and marketing?

The speakers who get booked the most aren't always the most talented, but they are the ones who stay top of mind. It's not enough to be great on stage; if no one remembers you when they need a speaker, you won't get hired. Staying known is just as important as becoming known in the first place, so how do you do it?

Some speakers make sure they're always visible by consistently putting out content: videos, blogs, interviews, or even books. Others take a smarter approach by repurposing what they already have. A sales speaker, for example, doesn't need to write a brand-new book for every group they address. Instead, they can tweak their existing content to be highly relevant to different industries, creating *Sales Strategies for Auditors* one year and *Sales Mastery for Lawyers* the next. It's the same expertise, just packaged to resonate with a new sector.

This isn't about churning out endless new material; it's about keeping your message fresh and relevant to the people who need it most. The speakers who do this well aren't just remembered; they're the ones who get booked again and again. You never know who's paying attention or when they'll decide to book you so you just need to keep showing up, keep sharing your expertise, and keep building relationships.

Known – How to get known: Action points

This is about marketing yourself, visibility, relationship building, so that you can get booked. Here's how to start building your reputation in the right way:

1. **Reach the right people.** Focus your marketing on bookers, event organisers and decision-makers who hire speakers.
2. **Stay in front of your market.** It takes seven to thirteen touchpoints to move someone from awareness to action. Be persistent and visible.
3. **Be where your audience is.** LinkedIn is essential, but also show up in the platforms where your audience is active.

4. **Give first, then ask.** Share useful insights, content and help. Let your value lead the conversation.

5. **Speak wherever you can.** Especially early on, say yes to events, panels and podcasts to build your presence and reputation.

6. **Build genuine relationships.** Maintain human connections – don't rely solely on automation or campaigns.

7. **Have a professional website.** It's your digital shop window and should clearly communicate what you do and why you matter.

8. **Use social media as a visibility tool.** Think of it as relationship-building, not just promotion. Share value regularly.

9. **Leverage traditional and podcast media.** Targeted features, interviews and guest slots can build authority and attract bookers.

10. **Commit to the process.** Getting known is an ongoing effort. Keep marketing even when you're getting booked.

$$B = \frac{(R+K+M+E)^v}{e}$$

4
Memorable (M)

'Always be yourself. Unless you can be Batman, then always be Batman.'
— Kevin Brown, entrepreneur and author

When I looked into why just 1% of the 4,489 speakers on LSB's roster got 80% of the bookings, it wasn't only because they were relevant and known, but also because bureau agents remembered them. When bookers were in a hurry and needed a quick recommendation, these were the speakers that came to mind first. Being great at what you do is important, but if people don't remember you, they can't book you.

In this chapter, we'll explore what makes a speaker truly unforgettable, from your content and delivery to how you engage beyond the speech itself.

What makes a memorable speaker?

Memorable speakers stand out. They are different. When a new brief comes in, speaker bureau agents will often brainstorm potential names. Who fits the bill? Who can they call straight away? The speakers who come to mind first are the ones who get booked most often.

When I ran my bureau, I saw this play out time and time again. Bookers don't always have the luxury of digging through endless lists, they go with the speakers they *remember*: the ones who made an impact, who delivered something remarkable, or who stayed in touch in the right way.

Being memorable isn't just about what happens on stage. It's about how you position yourself, the impression you leave behind, and how easy you make it for people to recall and recommend you.

> **TIP**
>
> A great way to be memorable to a bureau is to pass them an enquiry. If someone contacts you with a date you can't do or a topic that isn't a fit, rather than saying no, introduce the bureau as a good place to find an appropriate replacement. The bureau won't forget your recommendation and will do what they can to pay you back by finding you a gig you *can* do.

Be memorable for the right reasons

If you've ever watched ITV's *The X Factor* or *Britain's Got Talent*, you'll know Simon Cowell's blunt, no-nonsense judging style (he's clearly modelled it on me...). You might also recognise his go-to phrase: 'I'm going to remember you'; usually we're all thinking the same thing at home. Simon's judged versions of the show internationally, always doing the same thing – looking for the standout acts, the ones people will talk about long after the show ends. Key is to ensure that they're remembered for the right reasons, and that applies just as much to all off-stage communication as it does to what you do on stage.

Everything you do before and after a speech shapes how you're remembered. How do you communicate off-stage? How do you handle enquiries and briefing calls? Imagine having a reputation for being brilliant and charismatic on stage but coming across as flat, distracted, or unprepared in conversations with bookers. That can plant seeds of doubt. If you're uninspiring on a briefing call, bookers might wonder if you'll be the same on the day.

One speaker I worked with was highly regarded in his field, well-known, and charging high fees but he didn't do his own briefing calls, his wife did them for him. That simply doesn't work. For many clients, the briefing call is their first direct interaction with the speaker. It reassures them that everything they've shared with the bureau has been passed on and understood, and shows that the speaker is engaged, committed, and taking their event seriously. I told him I wouldn't work with him unless he handled his own calls, and that if Neil Armstrong, the first man on the Moon, could do his own briefing calls, then so can any speaker. He changed from that day forward and began joining every call himself, with his wife still present to take notes and follow up on any actions. Neil understood that preparation and professionalism weren't just about what happened on stage but in every interaction leading up to it, and now this speaker did too.

It's not just about briefing calls. How you show up at the event itself matters. Arriving late, flustered, or unprepared is far more memorable than anything you say on stage. Similarly, if you disappear straight after speaking, people remember that too. The speakers who stick around, engage with attendees, and add value beyond their talk are the ones that get booked again.

There are plenty of speakers I'll never forget, but not always for the right reasons. Some were terrible on stage, some were unprofessional off it, and some were just downright unpleasant. I'll share my top horror stories in the chapter on ego, but for now, let's focus on the kind of memories you *do* want to leave behind – the ones that make you bookable.

Be yourself

What makes *you* memorable? Everybody has something special, something unique to offer, and all I'm suggesting is leaning further into what that is for you.

It's always better to be yourself. If you've seen the 1996 Michael Keaton film *Multiplicity*, you might remember how each clone of the lead character became a little less sharp than the original. There's a great lesson here for speakers who copy someone else's material or style – it doesn't work. At best, they're forgettable. At worst, they're a bad karaoke version of the real thing.

There's only one version of you and being authentic is always the fastest route to being remembered, but sometimes speakers don't recognise what makes them stand out. A great example is Sarah Furness. I first came across her when she was speaking at a Professional Speaking Association event. The moment she started talking, I could see she had raw talent and commercial appeal. She had something special, but she wasn't leading with it. At the time, she was talking about using meditation and mindfulness to improve performance. Important, yes, but not what made her truly memorable.

What makes Sarah stand out is that she's a glamorous woman with a background as a combat helicopter pilot. That alone makes people sit up and take notice. During her career, she crashed not one, but three helicopters.

How many people can say that? Sarah's background and story sets her apart. Meditation and mindfulness are powerful tools, but they're not what makes her memorable. They're part of how she did what she did, not the reason people are drawn to her. Leading with her unique background makes all the difference.

It was a similar story with Holly Budge. Holly is an adventurer, a world-record-holding skydiver, and a conservationist working on the front lines of antipoaching initiatives in Africa. She's climbed Mount Everest, led expeditions through remote jungles, and worked alongside rangers tackling wildlife crime. In short, she has an extraordinary life story, but when Holly first came to me, she'd been given terrible advice: strip all of that out and only talk about speaking on her website. The thinking was that it would make her look more 'professional' but what it actually did was make her forgettable.

We put that right fast. Her website needed to showcase what made her unique: her adventures, her experiences, and the fact that she's out there in the world doing things most people couldn't even imagine. The result? She was quickly listed with new speaker bureaus and the bookings started coming in at the new higher fees we'd set for her.

What makes you different?

People don't just book speakers for their content. They book them for their stories, their experiences, and the unique perspective they bring. If you strip away what makes you different, you're making it harder for people to remember and book you.

Not everyone has a background like Sarah or Holly, but that doesn't mean you can't be memorable. Customer experience speaker Ken Hughes took a completely different approach. The first time I saw him speak, he was wearing a blue jacket and contrasting orange trousers. I genuinely wondered if he might be colour blind. When I asked him about his wardrobe, he smiled and said, 'Later, have a look at the attendees networking and see if you can spot me.'

After delivering his talk, he walked into the crowd. Surrounded by a sea of black, grey, and navy suits, he was impossible to miss, and that was the point. Until he spoke, he was just some guy in orange trousers, but once people had heard him, the blue jacket and orange trousers made him easy to find for follow-up conversations, potential bookings, and deeper engagement. He stood out, and that made him unforgettable.

Brad Burton tells us to own what makes us different. He is known for his no-nonsense, high-energy style. He wears t-shirts on stage, swears (when appropriate), and doesn't try to fit into the mould of a traditional corporate speaker, and that's exactly why he stands out. Too many speakers dilute their personality to appeal to everyone, but as Brad says: 'In the history of humanity, tell me one person whose style is for everyone. I'll wait.'

Being memorable doesn't have to mean having a jaw-dropping backstory; sometimes it's just about doing something different, something that makes you stand out in a sea of sameness. Whether it's a bold wardrobe choice, a distinctive speaking style, or a unique way of interacting with event attendees, embrace what makes you *you*.

> **TIP**
> An easy way to be memorable is to embrace your fashion sense and dress memorably.

The best speakers don't perform, they connect. They aren't acting or putting on a show; they're simply being themselves but just with the volume turned up a little. There are also times when just being yourself means daring to break the mould entirely.

Years ago, I came across Kjell Nordström and Jonas Ridderstråle, economists by profession, but you'd never guess it by looking at them or listening to them speak. Dressed in all black, with shaved heads, funky glasses, leather jackets, and skinny trousers, they looked more like rockstars than economists, and they spoke like no economists I'd ever encountered. Instead of citing predictable case studies and economic models, they talked about Britney Spears and porn. Their books had titles like *Funky Business*, *Karaoke Capitalism*, and even included a comic strip. They didn't just challenge economic thinking, they challenged what people expected an economist to look and sound like. That's what made them unforgettable. They weren't performing a version of what they thought an economist should be. They were fully and boldly themselves.

I've seen plenty of speakers who step onto a stage and instantly switch into 'speaker mode'. You know the type: rehearsed to a fault, with rigid delivery and gestures copied from someone else. They may tick boxes, but they don't stick in your memory.

What makes a speaker memorable is when they sound like a real person having a real conversation. When someone is natural, relatable, and authentic, I pay attention. I listen. I engage. Most importantly, I remember them.

Impact your audience

It is not enough just to speak to your audience – you want to leave them changed in some way by what you have said. There are various ways in which you can leave a mark on those who hear you, and we are going to consider how you make them feel, how you make them think, and what you make them do.

Making audiences feel

I feel good after watching Ken Robinson's TED talk, 'Do schools kill creativity?' Why? Because he's smart and makes me laugh. Ken was an incredibly memorable speaker. He told original stories laced with humour, and originality matters. We remember how we feel when we hear something fresh, something that makes us see the world differently. Sadly, he died in 2020, but his talks are still relevant.

At a recent event, I saw eight speakers back-to-back. How many said something I hadn't heard before or gave me a new take on something I already knew? One. That's the speaker I remember.

The most-booked speakers don't just inform; they take you on an emotional journey. Jaz Ampaw-Farr, who speaks on 'Resilience and Leadership', tells a tough story which has you laughing out loud one minute and wiping away tears the next. That's a real skill. Ranulph Fiennes, often called 'the world's greatest living explorer', does something similar. He delivers a dry, understated talk about his extreme adventures while casually showing horrific images of his injuries. The contrast makes it more powerful.

Not everyone needs to be funny, but every speaker needs to tell engaging stories. The best storytellers keep things simple.

Stephanie 'Steve' Shirley, a pioneering IT entrepreneur, is a great example. On the face of it, she breaks every 'rule' of speaking in her TED talk, 'Why do ambitious women have flat heads?': she sits down, uses cue cards, and doesn't move around the stage. Some speaker coaches would say that's not ideal, but it doesn't matter. She's compelling. She tells a story so well that you hang on every word. That's what makes a speaker memorable.

Making audiences think

Neil Armstrong could have had highly paid speaking engagements every day of the week. Instead, he was incredibly selective, accepting only a handful of invitations each year. Why? Because the content mattered to him. He wasn't a dynamic performer, but he was deeply thoughtful. Every speech was unique. He spent weeks tailoring each presentation, carefully choosing his words and crafting his stories. He didn't rely on being the first man on the Moon. He wanted to offer something more than just his celebrity status, and that's exactly what made him memorable.

There was also something else that made Neil stand out. No matter how many people had come to hear him speak, he would stay after his speech and personally shake hands with every single person who wanted to meet him. People would queue for the chance to shake hands with the first man on the Moon and he never rushed them. That moment of personal connection made the experience unforgettable.

Beau Lotto, a world-renowned neuroscientist, had a challenge. How do you take something as complex as perception and make it engaging? He knew that if people couldn't connect with his ideas, they wouldn't remember them, so we worked together on a simple but powerful promise: 'See differently to think differently'. Beau uses his own original optical illusions to prove his points, showing how our perceptions are shaped by experience and bias. His talks leave people questioning everything they thought they knew. It's an experience that stays with them long after they have left the room.

Mark Stevenson is another speaker who makes people think. He is a futurist who first became known for his optimistic outlook through his best-selling book *An Optimist's Tour of the Future* (Profile Books, 2012). That alone set him apart from other futurists, but he doesn't stop there. Mark researches his clients, studies their industries, and digs into what really matters to them. He does this to challenge their thinking. He doesn't just share ideas. He provokes audiences to rethink the assumptions they have held for years.

Being memorable isn't just about having an interesting topic. It is about making people think in a way that shifts their perspective. Whether it is through storytelling, science, or challenging ideas, the best speakers leave you with something you can't shake off.

Making Audiences take action

End clients, meeting professionals, and speaker bureaus are all looking for speakers who deliver real impact. If you can genuinely help people create change, you're far more likely to be remembered. This is especially true in the corporate world, where failing to adapt can be costly. Big business is littered with cautionary tales of companies that didn't evolve when they should have.

Taxi companies dismissed Uber as a passing trend but now it's taken over the industry. Traditional hotels didn't take Airbnb seriously, failing to see how consumer preferences were shifting towards unique, flexible accommodation. Even big retail chains underestimated the power of online shopping, leaving brands like Amazon to reshape how we buy. If these businesses had been more open to challenging their thinking, who knows what could have happened. Maybe they'd still be leading the market today. Speakers like Mark Stevenson and Beau Lotto specialise in shifting perspectives and helping businesses see what's coming before it's too late.

Change isn't just about business survival, though. On a personal level, people are always looking for practical, hands-on ways to improve. They want tools they can take back to work and use. As the saying goes, 'Insanity is doing the same thing over and over and expecting different results.' If you introduce a new approach that helps people, see, or do things differently, you'll make a lasting impact.

One speaker who has had a real effect on my life is Graham Allcott, aka the Productivity Ninja. Spend time with him, and you'll walk away with a list of simple but effective actions that will make you more productive. He taught me how to manage my to-do list, take control of my inbox, and prioritise my time. Whenever I slip back into bad habits, I go straight back to his book. Do I remember Graham? Absolutely, and when someone asks me for advice on productivity, he's the first name I mention.

It only takes one strong idea to stick. Jamil Qureshi tells us to shift our focus from what we want to do each day to who we want to be. Mel Robbins is known for her Five Second Rule: if you have an idea but don't act on it within five seconds, the moment passes and nothing changes. Simple, clear, and instantly applicable. Once you've heard Jamil's and Mel's concepts, they stay with you. That's true of all great speakers. Bookers remember the ones who leave a real impact, and if bookers remember you, you're already one step closer to getting into that top 1%.

You can take this even further by having a 'phrase that pays': a line so powerful it becomes synonymous with you, like Mel's Five Second Rule. Jaz Ampaw-Farr's messages are so impactful that she puts them on t-shirts, mugs, and even jewellery, which she gifts or sells. It's not just about branding; it's about reinforcing your message in a way that sticks with people long after your talk. What's your version of this? What's the phrase that sums up your message so well that people would want to carry it with them? If you can't articulate it immediately, your audience won't remember it, so confirm, clarify, and condense your message until you can.

Staying top of mind

If you position yourself as a trusted expert, one speech won't be enough. You want to build a relationship where they see you as someone they can turn to again and again. To do that, you need to stay at the top of mind.

One way to do this is with a small gift. Trust me, bookers like gifts. Ken Hughes has mastered this. He doesn't just send generic thank yous, he makes his gifts fun and unexpected. Instead of sending something at Christmas when everyone else does, he picks random dates like Halloween or Valentine's Day. His gifts are always playful. One year on St Patrick's Day, he sent me a pair of shamrock sunglasses. Completely ridiculous, but memorable. I particularly love the funny socks he sends. In fact, I'm wearing a pair as I type, which is exactly the point – I thought of him.

I remember working with Brendan Hall, who wanted to remind bureaus and past clients to book him. We came up with chocolate, because who doesn't love chocolate? We didn't just send *any* chocolate. Brendan found a chocolatier who made large, high-quality bars, too big to finish in one sitting (though I managed). The idea was that their size meant they'd sit on a booker's desk for a while, giving people plenty of chances to read the label wrapped around them. His bio, contact details, and key information were printed right there on the wrapper. Memorable? Absolutely. (You might want to make a note that I love chocolate. I can *always* eat chocolate, so if anyone wants to send me some, I promise I'll absolutely remember you.)

I will never forget my first ever booking. It was for Lawrie McMenemy, who was managing Southampton Football Club at the time. Wanting to appear professional, I didn't tell him it was my first until after the event. He later sent me a beautiful handwritten letter saying, 'I thoroughly enjoyed being your first.' That was nearly thirty years ago, and I still remember it though I have no idea where the letter is.

Philip Hesketh, a keynote speaker on the psychology of persuasion and influence, takes a similar approach. He sends handwritten postcards from his travels: greetings from Budapest/the Nile/New York/Paris. They aren't just standard postcards either. He personalises them through apps, featuring himself by a famous landmark or tourist attraction. It's a clever, funny way of saying thank you and staying memorable.

Phil also writes the best newsletter I've ever subscribed to. In fact, it's the only one I've *never* unsubscribed from. He sends it about once a month, so it doesn't feel overwhelming and it always contains something interesting about influence and persuasion. What makes it truly unmissable is that it's funny. Phil is hilarious, and he makes sure his newsletter is just as entertaining as he is on stage, because that's who he is.

Transformational speaker and humourologist, Paul Boross, does something just as simple but equally effective. Every time I booked him, he sent a personal thank you note, and every Christmas, I receive a card with a funny picture of him and his son dressed in outrageous outfits or caught in some silly situation. It always makes me laugh, and, of course, it keeps him top of mind.

A bit of effort goes a long way. In a world of emails and automated messages, taking the time to write something personal stands out, and when bookers remember you, they book you.

> **TIP**
>
> Thoughtful gestures like a handwritten note or a small, meaningful gift, keep you in a booker's mind. It's about the thought, not the cost, just keep it within bribery and corruption laws.

Your audience

You may have noticed a common theme running through all the advice in this chapter: it's not about you; it's about your audience.

Your audience's memories are the lens you need to look through as you build and maintain your speaker profile. It's their experience of you that determines whether you're remembered, recommended, and rebooked.

Ask yourself:

- Do they think I stand out?
- Is my content fresh, relevant, and original?
- Am I telling stories in a way that sticks with them?
- Do I make them feel something?
- Have I challenged the way they think?
- Will they remember me tomorrow/next month/next year?

Just as importantly, am I keeping in touch? Am I sending them something thoughtful, personal, or, ideally, chocolate? (Did I mention I love chocolate?)

If you can say yes to most of these, you're on the right track. Keep going; keep refining; keep making an impact.

Memorable: Action points

If you want to stand out and stay in people's minds, it takes more than just delivering a good talk. Here are ten practical ways to make yourself unforgettable:

1. **Be yourself.** Everyone has something memorable about them. Lean into your natural strengths and quirks rather than trying to imitate others. Make a list of what makes you unique and use it.

2. **Create real connections.** Audiences remember speakers who make them *feel* something. Focus on building a genuine connection rather than just delivering information. If this doesn't come naturally, practise.

3. **Master storytelling.** Great stories make messages stick. Develop your storytelling skills so you can take your people on an emotional and intellectual journey, not just deliver facts.

4. **Tap into emotion.** People remember how you made them *feel*. Go beyond logic and facts and look for ways to create an emotional connection that leaves a lasting impression.

5. **Make people think.** Fresh, thought-provoking ideas are memorable. Share insights that challenge assumptions or offer new perspectives, rather than repeating what they've heard before.

6. **Tailor.** A speech that feels personal and specific is always more memorable than something generic.

Do your homework and tailor your content accordingly.

7. **Give people something to act on.** Make sure delegates leave with a simple, actionable takeaway they can apply immediately.

8. **Be memorable off-stage too.** How you show up in meetings, emails, and phone calls matters just as much as your performance on stage. Bookers remember speakers who are consistently professional and engaging.

9. **Stay in touch.** Small, thoughtful gestures can keep you top of mind with bookers. A personalised touch makes you stand out.

10. **Put your audience first.** Always ask yourself, 'Is this meaningful to my audience?' When you focus on their needs, challenges, and aspirations, you naturally become harder to forget.

$$B = \frac{(R+K+M+E)^v}{e}$$

5
Easy (E) – Easy To Book

'Sometimes it's not about being the best candidate. It's about being the easiest.'
— Ross Bernstein, keynote speaker and author

Speakers who are easy to book and work with have a huge advantage. Event organisers have a lot on their plates and so they will often choose the speaker who makes their life easier over the one who is technically 'better' but more difficult to deal with. If booking you feels like hard work, you could be losing opportunities without even realising it.

Being easy isn't just about logistics. It's about reducing uncertainty and friction. Think about the way we use technology in everyday life. People shop on Amazon because it's quick and convenient, even if it's not the cheapest option. Uber changed the taxi industry by making travel stress-free: passengers know exactly when their ride will arrive, who's driving, and how much it will cost. The whole process is designed to remove hassle and risk.

As a speaker, why not aim to be the Amazon or Uber of the industry? The easier you make it for people to find you, book you, and work with you, the more likely you are to get repeat bookings. This variable of the formula is so important that, as with 'Known', I've given it two chapters: 'Being Easy To Book' and 'Being Easy To Work With'.

Even if you think you're already doing everything right, take a close look at these chapters. Sometimes, small details make all the difference. If you spot just one thing you could do better, it might unlock more bookings.

Be easy to find

First things first: your name. Be consistent across all platforms. If your name is Mike Carter, don't be Michael J Carter on LinkedIn, MJ Carter on YouTube, and MikeCarter.com on your website. Pick one version and stick with it. Once you've decided, buy your domain name, if available, and use that for your website and emails.

It still surprises me how many speakers don't tell people they speak. If you want speaking engagements, you need to make it crystal clear that's what you do. At the time of writing, LinkedIn is one of the first places bureaus and event organisers look for fresh ideas. Adding 'speaker' to your profiles helps. This makes it easier for bookers to find you instead of Mike Carter, the film director, or Mike Carter, the travel writer. If they're searching for speakers, make sure you show up.

I've seen several speakers use a clever LinkedIn tactic to highlight their bookability. They feature a post at the top of their profile with a strong testimonial and a clear call to action, something like, 'If you're looking for an engaging speaker, let's talk.' It's a simple but effective way to use testimonials to show credibility and make it easy for bookers to take the next step.

Now let's talk about your profile photo. Use the same image across all platforms: LinkedIn, YouTube, your website's main speaker page, etc. This helps with instant recognition. If someone sees you on LinkedIn and then checks out your website, they should immediately know they're in the right place. This is particularly important if your appearance changes frequently. If you regularly change your hairstyle or hair colour, make sure your main profile image remains consistent. A dramatically different look can make it harder for bookers to recognise you, especially if they've only seen you online.

> **TIP**
>
> Check your LinkedIn URL and make sure it is consistent. You can customise it; mine, for example, is simply www.linkedin.com/in/mariafranzoni

Making contact

One of my biggest frustrations when booking speakers was simply not being able to reach them quickly to check availability and fees. Time is money, and delays can cost you the gig.

Yachtsman Brendan Hall told me that 95% of his enquiries these days are via the website LiveChat because it's instant. Many bookers still use the phone, although if the booker is under thirty-five, they might prefer text or WhatsApp. Either way, they need a number to call.

I get that not everyone wants to put their personal mobile number online, but there are easy ways around it. I use a VoIP number for my business. It costs me about £5 a month and I've set it to go straight to voicemail with a personal greeting so callers know they've got the right person. Voicemails and texts get forwarded to my email, so if it's important, I can respond straight away. If it's a sales call, they rarely leave a message, and if they do, I can just hit delete.

EASY (E) - EASY TO BOOK

Here's something that really irritates me: when I call someone and the voicemail just repeats the number without confirming who they are. My first thought? Have I dialled the right person? I hang up, double-check, and call again. Not exactly a smooth start. What do I find even worse? When the voicemail says, 'Don't leave a message, send a text.' If I'm calling to book a speaker, I don't have time for that. I'd just move on to the next option. (I think I may just have given away that I'm over thirty-five.)

Back when I ran my bureau, I paid for a human messaging service which made life a lot easier. They'd take messages, screen calls, and if a call was urgent, they'd put it straight through to me. It was seamless and professional so this is something to think about if funds allow.

At the end of the day, speaking is a business, and businesses need to be easy to reach. If bookers struggle to get hold of you, they'll just go on to the next speaker on their list. It's as simple as that so make sure you're the first and the last number that they call.

Fees and availability

Most bookers reaching out need to know the answer to two simple questions:

1. Are you available?
2. What's your fee?

By the time they contact you, they've already done their homework: checked out your website, watched a video or two, and read your testimonials. They wouldn't be getting in touch if they weren't interested, but they need those two key pieces of information to proceed.

Some speakers put their fees on their website, but I don't recommend it. The moment you put a number out there, you risk shutting down conversations before they even start. A booker might assume you're too expensive when you could have offered a cheaper option if the gig appealed: a virtual session, a recorded talk, or even a workshop instead of a keynote. If they see £10,000 on your site but only have £5,000 available, they probably won't even bother reaching out, and you instantly lose the chance to explore what might have been possible.

While of course fees are important, the first thing bookers want to know is whether you're available, and they want that answer fast. If they can't get it quickly, they'll move straight on to the next speaker on their list.

Even if you don't have an immediate answer, just acknowledging the enquiry keeps you in the running. A quick 'Thanks for getting in touch, let me check my schedule' is better than silence. Having an up-to-date personal calendar is essential; don't rely on automated shared calendars alone as they don't always account for hold dates, travel time, or existing commitments properly.

EASY (E) – EASY TO BOOK

If you're not available, don't just say 'no' and leave it at that. Check if the event runs over multiple days, maybe there's flexibility. If not, suggest alternatives: a virtual session or a pre-recorded talk might still work for them, and being helpful now can put you at the top of their list for future events.

If it's an international booking, triple-check the time zones for virtual engagements and check travel time for in-person. Don't assume there's a direct flight or that the venue is anywhere near the airport. I've lost count of the times I've had to rescue a speaker who said 'yes' first and figured out the logistics later. If you're reading this, you know who you are…

Make yourself the easy choice

Having received the initial enquiry, at this point most speakers will pencil the date into their diary and sit back, waiting for the booker to get back to them. This is a risk: from the booker's perspective, they may be simply building a shortlist and putting together notes on why each speaker is a good fit. You want the booker to book you, but now you're relying on their memory to recall your preliminary conversation, your points, and whatever they can pull from your website. The problem is that you have no idea if you're the only speaker in the running or if you're up against five… or even forty. Yes, forty. I once worked with a client who thought forty was a shortlist. It was a total nightmare when it came to checking fees and availability.

Don't risk disappearing into the crowd. There are things you can do to protect against this. Speakers are often chosen by committee, so sending materials that can be easily shared is important. When we represented Jamil Qureshi, we would send a storyboard mapping out the scenes of his talk. It was a great way to help bookers visualise what he would deliver on stage. James Taylor sends a short video after calls, recapping the key points and showing his enthusiasm for the event, and Jaz Ampaw-Farr sends video at the point of enquiry. A recording of Jaz speaking to camera, reflecting back what the client is looking for and showing exactly how she can help. It's not polished or overproduced but it's powerful. Clients feel like they've already met her and are flattered by her interest and engagement in their project.

Whatever route you choose, make sure everything that might be needed to choose you is in the decision-makers' hands. The smoother you make their job, the better your chances of getting booked.

Give me patience but give it to me now!

This is my personal motto. You're welcome to borrow it.

I'm not a patient person at all, but in this business, you need to learn patience, or you'll spend most of your time frustrated. Sorry about that.

I've worked with many speakers who move into speaking expecting decisions to happen at the same speed as in their previous career, but speaking doesn't work like that. The expectation is that speakers will respond quickly, provide everything needed, and be ready to go when required, but bookers? They take their time. Even when the event is just around the corner. That's often because there isn't just one decision maker, and when there's a whole team involved, it takes time to get a final 'yes' or 'no'. Be prepared to fall into a holding pattern for a while: bookers will go quiet; dates will hang in the air. Don't panic and definitely don't let frustration show. Everyone is just doing their job.

You need to follow up, but without being pushy. Here's what we used to do in my bureau: when we pencilled a date in a speaker's diary, we told the booker that pencils expire after two weeks. That gave us a natural reason to check in: 'Would you like to renew the pencil, or shall we release the date?' It kept the conversation going and kept the speaker top of mind without feeling like we were chasing. If they needed more time, we'd agree to check in again in another two weeks.

This wasn't just about confirming the date. It was also an opportunity to catch up, find out how their event planning was going, and stay in the conversation. Sometimes, in that chat, we'd find out about other speakers they were considering, changes in the event, or even new opportunities. Staying engaged gave us a huge advantage over the competition who weren't following up. While they were waiting for a decision, we were strengthening the connection, making it far more likely that, when the time came, we were the people they felt most comfortable booking with.

A big part of being easy to book is understanding that decisions take time. Patience really is a virtue in this business. If you trust the process and don't get too emotionally invested in every single enquiry, you'll do better in the long run.

You will get 'no' more often than 'yes' to start with, but many of those initial nos will come back later. There are so many reasons why it might be a no this time, and most have nothing to do with your suitability. This business is a marathon, not a sprint. Stick with it.

Easy to book: Action points

Being a great speaker isn't enough; you also need to be easy to find and book. The smoother you make the process, the more likely bookers are to choose you. Here's how to remove friction and make hiring you a no-brainer:

1. **Be consistent.** Use the same name and title across all platforms so there's no confusion. Make it clear you're a professional speaker, don't assume people will just know.

EASY (E) - EASY TO BOOK

2. **Make contact simple.** Bookers don't have time to chase people. Have a clear, visible contact option on your website and LinkedIn. If you're not comfortable sharing your mobile number, use a VoIP line or professional messaging service.

3. **Respond quickly and clearly.** Availability, fees, logistics: have this information ready to go. Bookers move quickly and a slow or vague response can cost you the gig.

4. **Offer solutions, not just a no.** If you're unavailable or out of budget, don't just decline, suggest an alternative. Bookers remember speakers who are helpful.

5. **Follow up thoughtfully.** Never assume the booker will remember you. Send a clear, personalised follow up with relevant materials like testimonials, case studies, and speaking clips.

6. **Remember that you're one of many.** Bookers shortlist multiple speakers, not just you. Stay professional, be memorable, and don't take it personally if they 'go in another direction' (a favourite phrase used by bookers when they've booked someone else).

7. **Stay in the loop.** Don't just pencil in a date and wait. Proactively check in to see where they are in the decision-making process and whether you can help move things along.

8. **Minimise risk.** Bookers want safe, reliable choices. Show professionalism and responsiveness throughout the process so they feel confident hiring you.
9. **Be patient but present.** Bookings can take time, with multiple decision-makers involved. Stay professional and engaged without being pushy.
10. **A 'yes' is just the beginning.** Securing the booking is just the first step. Be ready to jump straight into the next phase of contracts, logistics, and prepping for a great delivery.

$$B = \frac{(R+K+M+E)^v}{e}$$

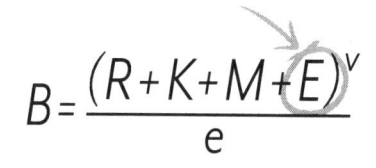

6
Easy (E) – Easy To Work With

'Do you leave people inspired, or inspired to leave?'
— Simon Lancaster, script writer and author

Being easy isn't just about getting booked. That's only half the job. Once you've got the yes, *then* the real work begins. This section is all about making sure you're easy to work with before, during, and after the event, and it all starts the moment you're booked.

They said yes: Paperwork perfection

Once you're booked, there's a whole process to go through to make sure everything runs smoothly. Organisers need your biography, high-resolution headshots, an introduction script, speech synopsis,

AV/travel/dietary requirements as quickly as possible. You don't want clients chasing you for materials or scrambling to get answers to basic questions, one way to make their lives easier is to have a dedicated section on your website just for event organisers. This can include the majority of what I've mentioned above, saving you and the clients time by reducing errors and minimising frustrating back-and-forth emails. It also makes you look professional and experienced, and can even save your life – quite literally in some cases. Marketing expert Andrew Davis, for example, has a peanut allergy. That's something event organisers need to know in advance, not when he's halfway through dinner. Details like this need to be available upfront.

Some speakers get this right from day one. Take Felicity Ashley, transatlantic rower, cancer survivor, and business founder. From the moment she stepped into the speaking world, she made herself incredibly easy to book. Her content, topics, and speaker information are laid out clearly and professionally online, so much so that I use her website as an example when training speakers. If you want to see how it's done, look at her website: www.felicityashley.com

The more you prepare in advance, the more professional you look, and the more likely you are to get booked again. The aim here is to build an enduring and mutually beneficial relationship, and first impressions count.

> **TIP**
>
> Be the speaker that organisers don't have to worry about. Event professionals have enough on their plate without speakers adding to their stress with constant requests and last-minute queries. Make yourself bookable by being calm, prepared, and self-sufficient.

Contracts

Every booking needs a contract. Some clients will send you their standard supplier agreement but these are rarely written with speakers in mind. Often, they're designed for builders, consultants, or other suppliers, and they won't include the specific terms you need as a speaker. That's why having your own contract is a good idea. It puts you in control, sets clear expectations, and avoids misunderstandings down the line.

One of the biggest areas where a contract protects you is payment terms. The industry standard is 50% to confirm the booking, the rest at least thirty days before the event; your cancellation terms should match those milestones. That way, you're not left in limbo if an event is postponed or cancelled. Some clients might try to negotiate, but if you have a contract, at least you're starting from your terms, not theirs.

Then there's the matter of intellectual property, particularly important when clients want to record your talk.

If a client does want to record your talk, they need your written approval including how, where, and for how long they can use it. You don't want to find your best material floating around online for free or, worse, being reused without your permission. Make sure you get final approval on any recordings so you can check the quality and ensure you get a copy for your own marketing.

I know contracts can feel like a hassle, especially if legal paperwork isn't your thing, but trust me, sorting this out upfront makes life easier for you and your clients. It stops awkward back-and-forth about money, prevents last-minute panic, and sets the tone for a smooth working relationship. Skipping this is like Paul McCartney not having a prenup when he married Heather Mills: painful, expensive, and completely avoidable.

> **TIP**
>
> You don't need to write a contract from scratch or pay a lawyer a fortune. There are great speaker contract templates available, including one on my website: www.mariafranzoni.me/bookability

Travel and accommodation

For many speakers, travel is one of the perks of the job. Seeing the world while getting paid to speak is a great lifestyle if you plan it properly, and like everything else, how you handle travel is another way to show you're easy to work with.

For organisers, travel and accommodation can be a major headache. Think about how many people they need to arrange flights, hotels, and transfers for: attendees, event staff, speakers. Then, just when they think everything is set, a speaker gets a last-minute booking or a change needs to be made, throwing all the logistics into chaos.

Most organisers book and pay for travel and accommodation directly, especially if they need you to be available before or after your talk. Many also have preferential rates with airlines and hotels, which can mean better deals and smoother logistics. If you need flexibility for last-minute changes, you would be better handling your own arrangements; a travel buy-out fee covering round-trip expenses can be a smart option. Just make sure it realistically covers your costs – too low and you're out of pocket; too high and you could price yourself out of the booking.

Some speakers include travel in their standard fee, making it even easier for bookers. Branding expert and best-selling author Martin Lindstrom was the first speaker I worked with who did this. For many years, Martin was based in Australia, but being Danish and well-known across Europe, many European events wanted to book him. A business-class flight from the other side of the world would have put a lot of them off, but by including travel in his fee, he removed that obstacle entirely. Most clients had no idea where he was based.

It didn't always work in his favour – sometimes he'd pay a big chunk of his fee towards flights; other times, the event was local, or followed on from a nearby location, meaning he kept more of his fee. Over time, it balanced out and, more importantly, it made him easier to work with.

> **TIP**
>
> A great way to calculate what you should add to your fee is to take last year's total travel spend and divide it by the number of events you did. Now you have an average travel figure, although, if you work with speaker bureaus, they will want a separate travel figure because only your speaking fee is commissionable.

Tom Peters, co-author of *In Search of Excellence: Lessons from America's Best-Run Companies* (Profile Business Classics, 2nd edition, 2004), is another example. His fee includes everything, right down to his hotel stay, with any special requirements arranged by his office in advance. That way, there are no last-minute surprises for organisers.

Whatever you do, avoid ending an event chasing outstanding travel costs. You don't want the last conversation you have with a client to be about expenses. Either invoice travel when you send your speaking fee invoice or have the client book and pay for everything upfront. If you do end up covering an unexpected cost, like grabbing a taxi because your arranged car didn't show, just absorb it. It's the cost of doing business.

> **TIP**
>
> Never travel on the last flight or train to an event: delays or cancellations can throw everything off. Plan to get there earlier and once you have, let the organiser know you've arrived safely. It's a small gesture that gives them peace of mind and makes you easier to work with.

Making it easy

An easy speaker is a huge attraction for bookers. Here are some ways in which you can make life easier for everyone involved.

Making AV easy

Tech can make or break a talk. Some speakers love it, layering in complex visuals, sound, and effects; others keep it as simple as possible. Whatever you do, make sure it runs smoothly, because you want your message to be talked about, not the tech that cut out or the slides that wouldn't load.

Bruno Marion, speaker, author, and self-styled 'futurist monk' relies heavily on AV to illustrate chaos theory, but he never leaves anything to chance. He travels with a full backup kit, including every adapter, cable, and spare device imaginable. If something fails, he can fix it on the spot; in fact, he's saved plenty of other speakers by having the right spare at the right time. It might seem extreme, but for Bruno, it means zero stress, no surprises, and no frantic searching for a missing cable.

At the other end of the scale, Jamil Qureshi takes the opposite approach. His AV requirements? A flip chart and some marker pens. That's it. If the audience is small, he works directly from the flip chart; if it's a big event, he just needs a camera pointed at the chart so the audience can see it on screen. No slides to send in advance, no compatibility issues, no tech headaches. Easy for him, easy for the client.

Paying attention to the details makes all the difference. Take rock band Van Halen's legendary 'no brown M&Ms' rule. Buried in their contract was a clause stating that if even a single brown M&M was found in the dressing room, they could cancel the show on the spot. Sounds like rockstar ego, right? Not at all. It was a quality control test. Their contracts were full of detailed safety and tech requirements for their complex stage setup. If the venue missed the M&M rule, what else had they overlooked? If brown M&Ms were spotted, the band immediately checked all the technical specs before going on stage. It saved them from potential disasters, and it's a good reminder that errors in small details often signal bigger issues. If something feels off in your tech setup, double-check everything before stepping on stage.

Always do a tech check on the day; strange things happen to slides between being sent and being uploaded by the AV team. Always treat your AV team well. They have the power to make you look and sound great, and they also talk to event organisers all the time. If they like you, they'll mention you; if you've been a nightmare to deal with, you can bet they'll be sharing that story too.

One final point: if a client asks for your slides in advance, send them by the deadline they've given you. Some clients need to check slides for compliance, branding, or translation, and late submissions can cause real headaches.

> **TIP**
>
> Always take your slides with you on a portable USB drive as a backup. Also use that drive to get a copy of any video footage taken of you on the day.

Getting paid

You've done the hard work, made yourself relevant, known, memorable, and bookable, but have you made it easy to get paid? If not, all that effort could end with you chasing money instead of enjoying it.

Make it simple. Accept payments in multiple currencies: If you're speaking internationally, at the very least, you should be set up to take USD, EUR, and GBP. While you're at it, offer a credit card option. You will, at some point, come across a client with a 180-day payment system (I kid you not), but those same clients can often pay instantly by card. Why wait six months if you don't have to?

Now let's talk invoices. Your bank details need to be clear and easy to find. This is not the place for tiny print, especially if you're dealing with international payments where account numbers can run to twenty-two digits. Also, don't forget to include your bank name and address. I lost count of the number of times I had to chase speakers for these details because my bank needed them for transfers. It delayed payments, created extra admin, and was completely avoidable. If your invoice is so small that it needs a magnifying glass to read, you're making life harder for the people paying you. Many companies still print, stamp, and manually check invoices before processing so if your bank details are microscopic, it slows everything down. Keep it simple, keep it readable, and get paid faster.

Then there are bank fees. If you're taking payments in multiple currencies, choose your account wisely. Some standard business accounts will eat into your fees with hefty charges. Wise is a great option – I use it myself and it's saved me a fortune in fees (and no, I'm not on commission, though I really should be).

Sort these things early and you'll get paid faster with fewer headaches. If the booking process, the logistics, and then the event itself all run smoothly, bookers will remember how easy you were to work with.

EASY (E) - EASY TO WORK WITH

> **TIP**
>
> Speed up payment with a credit card. If a client has a long payment process or delayed purchase order system, suggest payment by credit card instead. You'll often find that one of the event sponsors can pay this way, allowing you to be paid upfront or much faster. Just remember to add the card processing fees on top of your fee — they can be significant on higher-value bookings and shouldn't come out of your pocket.

If you have put the necessary time and effort into adequate preparation in advance, your time at the event should pass smoothly. Here are a few hints on how to make things easy – for yourself and others – during the event.

Be engaged

If it works for the event organiser, sitting in on a few sessions before you speak is a good move. It gives you a sense of the room, the discussions happening, and what's already been covered. A quick reference to something said earlier in the day helps create a good flow across the event and paints you as an interested and attentive participant.

Another way of demonstrating your engagement and investment in the event is illustrated by peak performance speaker Ross Bernstein. He likes to cast a member of the client's team as the hero of a story in his content. He does this is by doing his homework, finding out about the client organisation, learning about their team members, and discovering individuals that he can highlight. It is a gesture that makes him easy to remember.

Engagement doesn't stop when you step off stage. Delegates often have questions and making yourself available, whether during a coffee break, over lunch, or at an evening function, makes a big difference. If you're open to chatting, let people know. Jaz Ampaw-Farr has a fun way of introducing this: she says she will be staying to do a 'meet and greet' after her speech if anyone has questions.

Not big on networking? Me neither. No problem. Ask the organisers if they can introduce you to key people. They'll usually be more than happy to help and can make sure you're speaking to the right people, whether that's VIPs, decision-makers, or just the most interesting voices in the room.

> **TIP**
>
> A smart way to handle Q&A with a large audience comes from Paul McKenna. Instead of relying on roving mics, he had fixed microphones at the sides of the stage and invited people to queue up to ask their questions. It kept things organised, saved time, and ensured more people got to participate.

Be flexible

At some point, you'll deal with an organiser who needs to make schedule changes during an event which will affect you. This is more likely to happen if you're the closing speaker or scheduled later in the programme. People overrun and timings slip, and in that situation, you need to check in with the organiser. How can you help rather than add to the situation? Of course, they might be happy to go past the published end time and you can stick to your original timings, but they may ask you to cut your session down. I was recently asked to cut my slot at a conference by twenty minutes. I was naturally disappointed, but it wasn't about me. Fortunately, I had two versions of my session and it was easy for me to substitute the shorter slide deck without anyone knowing apart from me and the organiser.

You need to remain professional in the face of change. You are being paid to speak, and this includes adjusting your content while still delivering value, if required. You need to learn to restructure your presentations on the fly if that is what is asked of you. This doesn't mean speeding up and simply flicking through slides, and it certainly doesn't mean skipping content and saying, 'if only we had more time, I could tell you about…' This might be true, and it can be tempting to use it as a technique to sell a future booking, but I strongly recommend you avoid it. It can leave participants feeling short changed and organisers feeling publicly criticised.

It may be that events underrun or a speaker drops out and you end up being gifted extra time to fill. It pays to have extra stories, case studies, anecdotes, and other content up your sleeve in case you're asked to continue past your natural ending. Beau Lotto travels with three versions of his presentation: a presentation to fill the time booked, a shorter version, and a longer version. He can change immediately and with a smile, knowing he can provide content of various lengths at the drop of a hat.

> **TIP**
>
> Have more than one version of your speech ready in case you need to cut your time or speak for longer.

Be who they expect

Your clients and the bookers have a good idea of who you are and what you will present on stage; your audience does not. Getting the introduction right is absolutely fundamental in shaping how you are received. A strong introduction isn't just a list of achievements or a run-through of your biography; it should establish the relevance of your topic and why you are the right person to talk about it. Get it right, and those forty-five to sixty seconds will set you up for success.

Leave it to the organiser to write, and you risk things going horribly wrong.

> **TIP**
>
> Grab my template for a professional introduction: www.mariafranzoni.me/bookability

Robin Sieger told me about one of his toughest gigs, where the organiser didn't use his introduction script and instead introduced him by telling the audience they were about to hear a 'hilarious and totally motivating speech'. As he walked on stage, he could see the audience physically lean back, fold their arms, as though to say, 'OK funny man, make me laugh.' Not exactly the warmest welcome, but Robin handled it brilliantly. As the organiser walked off, he stepped into the middle of the stage, paused, and said, 'Wow, after an introduction like that, even *I* can't wait to hear what I'm going to say.' It got a laugh, but he still had to work hard over the next five minutes to shift their focus from the introduction to his actual content. Not ideal.

> **TIP**
>
> Send your intro digitally in advance so it can be uploaded to an autocue/comfort monitor or shared with the emcee and take a copy with you just in case the emcee hasn't got it on the day.

In Robin's words, 'Your speech starts from the first word of the introduction as it sets the expectation. Therefore, you need to control it. This is so important that I often tell speakers to print their introduction on coloured paper and laminate it. That way, they can spot it in the organiser's hand from a distance, and because it's laminated, it's harder for anyone to make last-minute edits. Your introduction is the first impression of you so make sure it's one that works in your favour.

Be engaging

When you are on stage, being easy to listen to really matters. I can't tell you how many so-called expert speakers have left me puzzled and asking, 'What was that?' as they draw to a close. The saying is true: 'It's not what you say; it's the way you say it.' A clear, logical structure that guides the listener is a must. You need to create a roadmap that makes it easy for people to follow your message, with a strong beginning, an engaging middle, and a memorable close. It doesn't matter how experienced you are, you can always improve your structure.

It's increasingly likely you'll be speaking to people for whom English isn't their first language, so as well as having good structure, you need to control your pace, allow for natural pauses, breathe, and let people catch up with you. It is easy to slip into the habit of speeding through your content, especially if you're doing it regularly, but each new group is hearing it for the first time.

It's also helpful to avoid industry jargon, colloquial language, or slang. I'd also steer away from swearing and expletives, unless you are Bob Geldof, who can get away with it, or Gary Vaynerchuk, who has made it part of his brand. There will be people who switch off if they hear swearing; I'm one of them. It pays to be polite and respectful generally.

The speakers that I have always found easiest to listen to are those who add a variety of stories to illustrate their points and use humour. It means not taking yourself too seriously and sharing experiences that may raise a smile. My go-to person when it comes to advice on humour is Emmy Award-winning writer Beth Sherman. Her mantra is that 'truth is funny'.

If you think about your favourite comedian, they may well rely on observational humour, telling stories from real life. You can do the same. Humour makes people listen. It helps them relax, pay attention, and remember what you said. Studies show we're more likely to retain information that makes us smile; this is known as the Humour Effect.[3] Relevant, well-placed humour or light-hearted observation doesn't just lift the room; it also helps ideas stick by triggering the

---

3   Kieth A Carlson, 'The impact of humor on memory: Is the humor effect about humor?', *HUMOR*, 24/1 (2011), 21-4. https://doi.org/10.1515/humr.2011.002

brain's reward system. You don't need to be a stand-up comic, but weaving in appropriate humour will make your message more engaging and memorable.

Storytelling expert Mark Leruste suggests thinking of your personal experiences as a 'vending machine of stories', ready to dispense the right one for the right audience. He uses a simple storytelling structure – context, connection, conclusion – or as he puts it: 'Tell me, Take me, Teach me.' He reminds speakers that the most powerful stories are the ones that make the audience feel seen. You don't need dozens, just a few well-chosen stories from which you can select the relevant ones and adapt, depending on who's in front of you.

Be reliable

I want to end this chapter with the best bit of business advice I have ever been given. This advice will make you incredibly easy to work with.

I asked 'Persuasion and influence' speaker Philip Hesketh for tips when I first set up my speaker bureau. My question was, 'What should I do to be successful?' He said, Always do what you say you are going to do.' It's such simple advice and seems obvious but the reason he shared this is because so few people do. You'll notice this now that I've brought it to your attention and it will irk you.

As a speaker, if you say you're going to send your slides in advance on a certain date, do it; if you say you're going to be there early, be there early; if you say you're going to network, network; and if you say you are going to use humour, use humour. If you deliver what you promise, every time you speak, you'll be the definition of easy to work with.

Easy to work with: Action points

I've summarised ten actions that will make you a dream to work with before, during and after any event:

1. **Prepare speaker resources.** Prepare all the information a booker might need in advance, such as biographies, AV requirements, and even dietary or other information.

2. **Be clear on travel arrangements.** Decide whether you'll handle travel yourself or opt for a buyout fee. Ensure this is clearly communicated to organisers.

3. **Have a standard contract.** Use a speaker contract template and ensure it is appropriately personalised with essential clauses, including payment terms, intellectual property rights, and recording permissions.

4. **Streamline payment options.** Offer multicurrency invoicing, credit card payments, and provide clear, concise bank details to avoid delays.

5. **Double-check your AV.** Share your detailed technical needs upfront, carry backup equipment if necessary, or simplify your setup and go low tech.

6. **Be helpful on the day.** Notify organisers of your arrival and stay approachable for last-minute changes or needs. Be part of the answer, not the problem.

7. **Be adaptable to change.** Be prepared for event plans to go awry. Have multiple versions of your presentation to hand so you can quickly respond to new instructions.

8. **Engage with the audience.** If you can, attend other sessions, reference event themes, and connect with attendees throughout the event, including Q&As and networking sessions.

9. **Speak well.** Structure your content well and use stories and humour to make your speech easy to listen to. It is generally best to avoid swearing and potentially contentious or triggering language.

10. **Keep your promises.** Always follow through on what you say you'll do, from submitting materials on time to delivering a polished, engaging performance.

$$B = \frac{(R+K+M+E)^V}{e}$$

7
Value (V)

> 'You are not being judged, the value of what you are bringing to the audience is being judged.'
> — Seth Godin, entrepreneur, speaker and best-selling author

You've made it this far – well done. You've mastered relevance, made yourself known, become memorable, and made life easy for bookers. Now comes the real difference-maker: Value. Value isn't just another variable in the formula, it's a multiplier.

When a booker hires you, they're taking a risk. Their reputation is now tied to how well you perform and the impact you create. If you deliver real value, not only does the audience benefit, but the person who booked you gets the credit for choosing wisely. Make them look awesome, and that's success, because a happy booker is a repeat booker.

Get value right and, in time, you'll find that you're no longer squeezed into the client's budget; instead, they're working to yours. Let's break down what value really means in the speaking business, starting with how it's perceived.

Perceived value

Value is tricky because it's often subjective and sometimes even contradictory. Take my favourite perfume. It costs £120 for 100 ml. That's a lot, especially when you consider the ingredients cost around £5 (according to Google), but I'm not just buying scent, water, and alcohol – I'm buying an experience. It's a confidence boost, a touch of luxury, and a reflection of my personality. That's perceived value. If I could pick up the same bottle at the pound store, would I still see it as special? Probably not.

The same applies to speakers. Scarcity can create value: a speaker who does fewer engagements can be seen as exclusive and more desirable. At the same time, visibility also builds value: if a speaker is everywhere, it creates confidence. If so many others are booking them, they must be good, right? This is why perceived value isn't fixed.

VALUE (V)

Neil Armstrong is a great example of using scarcity to maintain value. When I worked with him, he only accepted a handful of speaking engagements per year. He didn't want to be booked just because he was famous; he wanted to be the right choice. That meant I had to go deep with clients to understand why they wanted to book him and whether their event was truly the right fit. Only then would he say yes. On the other hand, speakers like Jamil Qureshi and Ross Bernstein take the opposite approach: they are highly visible. If you look at their LinkedIn feeds, they're always speaking somewhere. As well as creating confidence that they are good, it creates FOMO: 'If other companies are booking them, we should too.'

Perceived value isn't static, it's something you can shape. A strong online presence, a well-designed website, a high-quality showreel, and consistent professional messaging all help. Testimonials and case studies that showcase client outcomes can significantly enhance credibility. Branding also plays a huge role. It's not just about logos or taglines, but how you position yourself in the market.

Perceived value might get you booked but actual value is what gets you rebooked. Overselling and underdelivering can damage your reputation, but if your impact matches or even exceeds expectations, you build trust and long-term success. Perceived value is also context-dependent.

Understanding what your booker values is crucial. Whether your perceived value comes from scarcity or visibility, what ultimately matters is delivering real impact.

What's in it for your customer?

When I work with new speakers, the first thing I ask is, 'What makes you bookable? How would I sell you?' If, as a speaker, you can't articulate that clearly, neither can anyone else.

Many speakers focus on what they do rather than what they solve. I've seen so many speaker websites packed with credentials and impressive presentations, but they miss the all-important 'So what?' factor. Your potential clients aren't lying awake at night wondering about your speaking style or your background. They're thinking about their challenges, their teams, their outcomes.

Your testimonials shouldn't just say you were great, they should showcase the difference you made. Your case studies shouldn't just list where you've spoken, they should highlight the problems you've helped solve. Nobody cares who you are or what you talk about until they know you understand their problems. Your value isn't in your words, it's in the transformation you create. It's about how your talk moves the way people think, feel, or act. It's about the problems you solve, the changes you create, and the impact that remains long after you've left the stage.

What are you actually worth?

When a booker is deciding whether to bring you in, they're not just looking at the fee – they're thinking about what's going to change as a result of you being there.

Yes, there's the cost of hiring you. But there's also the value you bring – to the event, to the people in the room and to the business afterwards. A good booker will weigh those up.

So, the real question becomes: what's different because you've spoken? What mindset shifted? What action was sparked? What ripple effect did you start?

If you can answer that clearly, you're far more likely to be seen as worth booking – and worth paying properly for.

Expertise, reputation and transformation

Let's answer the above questions by breaking value down into three elements.

The first of these is your **expertise**. What qualifies you to speak? What's your experience, knowledge, and credibility? This isn't about being the world's leading expert (though that helps); it's about having real, relevant expertise. Bookers look at this first because it's tangible, they can measure it against their needs.

Next, bookers consider your **reputation**. Do you come highly recommended? Do you have strong testimonials and case studies that demonstrate actual results? Are you known for being easy to work with? Creativity speaker James Taylor, for example, showcases detailed case studies on his website, highlighting who his clients are, what they needed, how he helped, and, most importantly, what outcomes they achieved.

Finally, bookers turn to the third element, and the best part of this one is that the third element of value is open to everyone, and it's the most powerful: **transformation**.

This isn't about changing the world in one speech – that's unrealistic – but sometimes transformation can be as simple as raising the energy in a room full of tired executives; helping a team see their challenges in a new way; or giving a sales team a small but effective tweak that leads to more closed deals.

You don't need to bring earth-shattering changes, just change that is meaningfully useful. Your expertise gets you noticed; your reputation gets you booked; but it's your ability to create transformation that makes you unforgettable and keeps those high-paying clients coming back.

From catalyst to long-term value

A speech is just the beginning. Think of it as lighting a match – it sparks new ideas, opens up possibilities, and gets people excited about change. If it's going to turn into something lasting, that initial flame needs fuel. If you want to create real impact, you need to go beyond the keynote. The most successful speakers understand they're not just delivering a talk; they're starting a transformation. Jamil Qureshi puts it well: it's like creating *mini muscles*. That first session in the gym might feel energising, but real change requires ongoing effort, the right guidance, and progressive challenges.

Too many speakers stop short of their full potential. They deliver an inspiring message, get great feedback, and walk away thinking the job is done. In fact, if you've just helped an audience recognise an important challenge or opportunity, they'll naturally have questions, things like:

- What next?
- How do we implement this?
- Where do we start?

The most successful speakers don't just show up, deliver a speech, and leave. They embed themselves into their client's world, identifying challenges before they even step on stage.

For example, a customer experience expert might start by auditing the client's current approach, pinpointing areas for improvement, and tailoring their speech to address those specific gaps. After delivering their talk, they provide a structured portfolio of follow-up activities, tools, and ongoing strategies. They're not selling from the stage; they're positioning themselves as a long-term solution provider. The result? Some clients start with a single speech and go on to invest six figures in extended programmes.

This approach works because it recognises a simple truth: one speech, no matter how brilliant, won't solve complex organisational challenges. If, instead, you position yourself as an expert who speaks, rather than just a speaker, you create opportunities for ongoing value through additional content, tools, frameworks, or programmes.

Consider what happens after your speech. To identify opportunities to expand and develop the worth of your offering, ask yourself:

- Are you providing tools or guides to help implement your ideas?
- Could you offer follow-up videos or resources?
- Are you available to answer questions or provide clarification?
- Have you created a pathway for deeper engagement?

Your real value isn't just in what you say on stage, it's in how you help your clients turn that initial spark into sustainable change. Get this right and you're no longer just another speaker, you're an indispensable partner in their success.

Prove your value

How do you prove your value as a speaker? Sometimes, you might have hard data at your fingertips: industry benchmarks, reports, or figures that back up your impact, but in my experience, that's rare. Most speakers deal with human performance, things like attitudes, frustrations, hopes, and emotions, which are much harder to measure.

One way to prove your value is by creating a baseline and measuring change. Beau Lotto and Penny Mallory are two speakers who do this particularly effectively. Beau Lotto measures how creative an organisation is before and after his talk, giving clients clear, tangible data to demonstrate the change. Penny Mallory does the same with mental toughness. She presents the results as 'group toughness scores', showing exactly what's changed. Both speakers provide measurable proof of their impact, making it easier for event organisers and speaker bureaus to see the value of their investment. It's a simple yet powerful way to stand out as a speaker who delivers real, trackable results.

Another way is to use surveys. There's various software available that allows you to survey participants live during your presentation. This is incredibly powerful, not only for demonstrating value but also for capturing new contacts. If your survey includes an opt-in, it's an easy way to grow your email list with engaged members who are already interested in your content. Surveys aren't just about proving impact, they help you identify more work opportunities beyond the speech.

Many clients need to justify the Return on Investment (ROI) of an event, especially when spending big on a speaker. Having clear, measurable outcomes helps them prove the value of their investment, not just to their teams but to leadership and stakeholders. If you can provide that, you make their job easier (which means they're more likely to bring you back).

If you don't have hard data, you can use anecdotal evidence, which can be just as powerful. One way to do this is to ask the right questions before and after your talk. You don't have to use software or apps to capture feedback. Consider these two examples:

- Anna Hemmings, Olympic and world champion kayaker-turned-speaker, hands out a double-sided printout at the end of her talk. One side has her contact details, the other a question asking participants what they got from her session and what action they will take.

VALUE (V)

- Adah Parris, futurist and consultant, gets participants to write postcards to their future selves. A few months later, she posts them back with a simple question: 'Did you follow through?' It's a clever way to reinforce the message long after the talk has ended.

Proving your value isn't just about what happens on stage, it's about what changes afterwards. Find a way to track that change, and you'll stand out as a speaker who delivers real, measurable impact, while creating new opportunities for future work for yourself.

Drilling down into the detail

How then should you address the gap between perceived value and actual value? It's important to fully scope out any speaking opportunity before preparing your speech and without making assumptions. This means having a detailed conversation with your client and taking a deep dive into their views. What matters to them? What are their goals? What problems do they have? What transformational change would they count as success? What do they perceive as valuable? It's important, as you look for answers, to talk to the most useful arbiter of value. For speakers, it is the person who booked you. They're paying for you, and they will be assessing the results.

> **TIP**
>
> If you'd like to go deeper into scoping, check out Mary's critical questions, available on my website: www.mariafranzoni.me/bookability

Customised or signature content

As a speaker, one of the biggest decisions you'll make is whether to focus on signature content, a talk that stays mostly the same each time, or customised content, which is tailored for each event. There's no right or wrong approach so choose what aligns best with your strengths and what your clients value.

Take Ranulph Fiennes. When people book him, they expect stories of Arctic and Himalayan adventures, overcoming frostbite, navigating impossible terrain, and pushing human limits. That's what they're paying for. He might tweak 20% of his talk to fit a theme like leadership or resilience, but the core of his speech remains the same. It works because he's booked for the experience and credibility he brings.

On the other hand, some speakers customise extensively. Futurist Rohit Talwar is known for his deep tailoring to the client's industry and current business context, spending three to five days researching and designing every talk before he steps on stage. This can include elements such as multiple interviews with attendees, a virtual leadership roundtable, and participant surveys. His clients don't just want insights about the future; they want insights about how to navigate *their* future. This level of customisation takes significant time and effort so it needs to be factored into pricing and availability. The advantage? Clients who value this level of detail and personalisation are usually willing to pay well for it.

Then there's a middle ground – structured flexibility. Jamil Qureshi has a signature framework based on eighteen psychological principles, each tied to a performance-related lesson and story. When he speaks, he selects the most relevant principles for each client during the briefing call, allowing him to tailor his talk while working within a tried-and-tested structure. It's an efficient way to adapt content without reinventing the wheel.

Think about whether you should focus on a signature talk, tailor every speech to each client, or find a balance that works for you.

Value and fees

When starting out, many speakers set their fees based on time and expenses. They pick a day rate, add a mark-up, and work from there. Your fee shouldn't just reflect time; it should also reflect your expertise, reputation, and the transformation you deliver. In fact, you can't confidently set a fee until you can clearly articulate these three factors, especially the last one. If you can't explain the outcome you create, how can you expect clients to put a high value on it? If what you offer isn't seen as urgent or important, it will always be difficult to charge high fees, but when your expertise directly addresses a pressing need, your price starts to make sense.

I've noticed some clear patterns when it comes to fees. Certain subjects attract higher fees than others; for example, innovation beats creativity, in my experience. Speaking to senior executives tends to attract higher fees than speaking to junior employees. It's also a common misconception that bigger audiences mean bigger rates. A small, high-level boardroom session can be far better paid than speaking to thousands. Internal staff events and external client events also tend to have different pricing structures.

There's no universal rate card. Instead of searching for a magic number, focus on understanding your value, being crystal clear about the problems you solve, and knowing the market you want to serve. The right fee is the one that reflects your worth.

The psychology of pricing

Pricing is more than just a number, it's about positioning. Your fee shapes how bookers perceive you. Too

VALUE (V)

low, and you seem inexperienced; too high, and you risk pricing yourself out. Understanding pricing psychology helps you strike the right balance.

- **Anchoring matters.** Bookers compare fees. If they see a £15,000 speaker first, your £5,000 fee may seem budget, but if they start with £3,000, you look premium. Tiered pricing – keynote only, keynote plus workshop, etc – can help frame your value.

- **Price signals quality.** Clients often equate higher fees with better speakers. A 10K speaker is assumed to deliver more impact than a 2K one. A low fee raises doubts: are you inexperienced? A strong price, backed by results, reassures bookers.

- **Scarcity creates demand.** Speakers who are in demand charge more. If your calendar is full, bookers are more eager to secure you. Some speakers increase fees as availability drops, reinforcing exclusivity.

- **Use contrast to your advantage.** Offering a high-ticket option, like a 50K programme, makes your 15K keynote seem great value. Without contrast, bookers lack a reference point.

How you communicate your fee matters just as much as the number itself. If you hesitate or sound unsure, it can weaken the perceived value of your offering, but if you state your fee with confidence and link it to the results you deliver, it reinforces your credibility and professionalism. Be intentional about how you present it. If you're struggling check out David Newman's salt and pepper exercise from his book, *Do It! Speaking* – it's brilliant. See the recommended reading section for more details.

If you want more tailored advice, that's best explored in a one-to-one conversation. If in doubt when starting out, take former hostage negotiator Chris Voss's advice and let the other side go first by asking what their budget is.

> **TIP**
>
> If you get booked ten times without anyone questioning your fee or trying to negotiate you down, it may be time to increase it.

The power of value

As a speaker, if you deliver exceptional value, it makes the individual who booked you look brilliant for choosing you. Putting on events, exhibitions and conferences is hard work and can cost huge amounts of money. It's risky and stressful too – a lot of things can go wrong – so imagine how good it feels to have a decision rewarded with a positive outcome.

Over-delivering by doing more than you promise is a great gift to pass on. In fact, I am convinced sharing real, genuine value makes the business of speaking more positive for everyone. Beyond money, it makes you, and everyone involved, feel great. That is why I use 'V' as a multiplier in my formula. Value is the most powerful bookability variable of all.

Value: Action points

I have summarised ten action points that will help you deliver real value throughout your speaking career:

1. **Fear indifference.** 'So what?' is the worst feedback a speaker can hear. Strive to always make a genuine difference and, once you do, tell the world about it.

2. **Know your worth.** Make sure you can articulate the value of your expertise, your reputation, and the transformational change you deliver. Only then can you begin to put a price on it.

3. **Value is subjective.** Use pre-event and scoping conversations to deep dive into your client's goals to understand what they value in a speaker. You may be surprised.

4. **Be a catalyst.** Encourage audiences to think of a challenge or opportunity in a new way. Be

realistic about what you can achieve from the stage, though. A spark will do it.

5. **Be more than a speaker.** Present yourself as an expert who adds value after any event. Help clients navigate from A to B by offering actionable steps, models, frameworks, and tools.

6. **Gather and share feedback.** Collect audience and client comments, takeaways, commitments, and success stories. Use them as testimonials and include them in case studies.

7. **Choose your content style.** Decide whether to specialise in signature content, customised content, or a mix of the two. Assess how that impacts on your value to bookers.

8. **Don't base fees solely on time or expenses.** Align your fees with the value you provide, not with your costs. Raise your rates periodically, especially if you're consistently getting work.

9. **It's always about the audience.** The ultimate arbiter of value is the person who pays the bill, but they will check with their audience, so never forget it's all about them.

10. **Over-deliver.** Make your booker look good and everyone feel good by doing more than is expected of you.

$$B = \frac{(R+K+M+E)^V}{\boxed{e}}$$

8
Ego (e)

'Be a diva onstage, and a delight offstage.'
— Lee Warren, sales and communication speaker

I'm very fond of Lee Warren's quote. When I asked him for permission to use it in this book, he expanded on the idea, explaining that when you're on stage, the spotlight is on you, and you have to be good. However, the moment you step off stage, you need to turn the spotlight 180 degrees and focus entirely on your client. I completely agree, but I'd add one more layer to this. Even when you're on stage, though the spotlight is on you, it's still all about the audience. I know I'm repeating myself here, but I really cannot stress this enough.

In the same way that value is a multiplier, ego is a denominator. If left unchecked, ego expands, and the bigger it gets, the more it shrinks your bookability. You can't argue with the maths. The challenge is that this can happen without you even noticing. A few too many standing ovations, a little too much deference from bookers, and before you know it, you start believing the hype. The moment you forget that your role is to serve, you become harder to work with, and that's when bookings start to dry up. The speakers who get booked over and over again? They master this balance. Command the stage but stay humble off it. It's that simple.

Confidence

Most people don't think about their ego. It operates in the background, shaping behaviour without us realising. For speakers, there's a fine line between healthy confidence and off-putting overconfidence, but it's not always obvious when you've crossed it. A little too much self-belief can tip into arrogance, and arrogance loses bookings.

This industry talks, a lot. That's hardly surprising given it's full of speakers. This means that word of bad behaviour spreads fast. It might not seem fair but it's reality: news of a speaker being difficult, demanding, or dismissive will reach bookers far faster than praise for doing a great job.

Now, I know you're expecting some juicy stories – don't worry, I've got plenty – but if you're hoping for names, I'll have to disappoint. Having worked as an agent and in a bureau, my job has always been to promote speakers, not expose them, and I'm not about to break that habit now. That said, if you read carefully, you might just be able to work out who I'm talking about. I'll leave that part to you. If stories of unchecked egos don't interest you, feel free to skip ahead. Honestly, the lesson is simple: ego won't be an issue if you just... behave well.

Let's be clear, confidence is essential. Every speaker I've mentioned in this book so far knows their value, delivers with skill, and makes a powerful contribution to any event they're booked for. That doesn't happen by accident. It takes confidence, not arrogance, just a steady belief in what you bring to the stage.

We've all seen someone on stage who clearly doesn't feel comfortable up there. You can sense their nerves, you start to worry for them, and suddenly the whole room feels nervous. No booker wants to risk putting someone on their stage who might crumble under pressure, so where does healthy confidence come from? The answer is simple: preparation, practice, and repetition. The more you speak, the better you get. The best speakers weren't born great, they put in the work, and when you've done the work, you don't need to force confidence. It shows.

Brad Burton didn't set out to be a speaker. When he started 4Networking, he had to speak at events because no one else would. The first few times, he was terrified, but he kept going. Over time, people started telling him he was 'motivational' and 'inspirational', and eventually someone asked him to keynote at an event. Brad says that you don't become confident by waiting to feel ready. Confidence comes from repetition. You have to put in the reps, whether that's speaking at networking events, running webinars, or even just talking to people one-on-one.

This does introduce a dilemma. If building confidence is good, how do you know if you've crossed the line from healthy confidence into damaging ego? One of the biggest red flags is an unwillingness to adapt. I've seen plenty of speakers become difficult to work with because they refuse to adjust their style or content to suit an event. It's easy to convince yourself that you know best, especially if you've been speaking for a while and have strong opinions about what works, but if you dig your heels in and refuse to change, that's not confidence. That's ego.

Being defensive and inflexible undermines your value. How you respond to feedback matters. If a client suggests something and you dismiss it outright, they're going to feel ignored, and that's a fast way to lose bookings. Clients don't need you to agree with everything they say, but they do need to feel like they've been heard.

There's another way an overinflated ego can show up that makes a speaker difficult to work with, and that is often manifest through unrealistic, inappropriate or unnecessary demands. An example might be demanding that an elite, high-end masseuse be flown in before you'll even *consider* speaking. This is one way to guarantee you won't be booked again, and yes, this really happened. Most cases aren't that extreme but even something as seemingly insignificant as refusing to attend a sound check or skipping a technical rehearsal can come across as diva-like behaviour. Events are a team effort and if you make life difficult for the organisers, they won't be in a rush to bring you back.

Confidence gets you booked. Ego gets in the way.

Behaviour matters

You can have the most fabulous speech and on-stage presence, but if your behaviour before and after is compromised, this will impact your bookability. Fundamentally, you are the product; everything you do, from the moment of first contact to the last, will contribute to the overall value of that product.

First names and first impressions

When I started in the industry, Alex Krywald, visionary founder of CSA Celebrity Speakers, gave me a piece of advice that has stuck with me ever since – always use first names. His reasoning was simple: everyone answers to their first name and it immediately creates parity between you, the client, and the speaker, making conversations more natural and negotiations smoother.

Take Neil Armstrong, who I often mention because he genuinely left a huge impression on me. Despite being one of the most famous people on the planet, he was perfectly happy for everyone to call him Neil. Ranulph Fiennes does the same; he doesn't insist on being called Sir Ranulph, he quickly puts people at ease with a simple, 'Just call me Ran.'

For speakers with titles, Doctor, Professor, Sir, or Dame, for example, it's worth considering the impact of using it when deciding how to introduce yourself. Being booked to speak already signals that your expertise is valued. While some people (especially in fields like politics or the military) appreciate formality as a mark of respect, in other settings, insisting on the use of your full title at all times can create unnecessary distance.

Whether you prefer formality or a relaxed approach, the goal should always be to make everyone feel at ease. A strong relationship built on mutual comfort and respect will take you much further than any title ever could.

TIP

People *will* know who you are – you're listed in the event programme and the marketing materials – but introducing yourself as you would in any other setting makes a big difference. A simple, 'Hi, I'm [your name], it's great to meet you,' paired with a friendly handshake sets the right tone and leaves a lasting impression.

Business versus pleasure

A speaking career can mean exciting travel and staying in glamorous places, but it's still a job, and a job requires professionalism. Don't be like one of my celebrity clients who enjoyed the perks a little too freely and – look away now if you're easily scandalised – slept with the event organiser's assistant, twenty years his junior. If there were such a thing as The Ten Speaking Commandments, Commandment Number One would be 'Thou Shalt Not Sleep with the Client.' It's one of the fastest ways to damage your reputation and lose future bookings.

I still remember how uncomfortable it was calling the next day to get feedback on the event, only to hear nothing about the talk, just about the speaker's nocturnal activities. When I confronted the speaker, he brushed it off as insignificant but the damage was done. The bureau lost the client, I stopped recommending him, and he didn't get rebooked until someone specifically requested him. Even then, I made sure the event didn't require an overnight stay.

The same applies to all kinds of unprofessional behaviour: making inappropriate jokes, being rude to junior staff, or overindulging at the hotel bar. I've seen it all, and none of it helps a speaking career. What you do in your own time is your business, but when you're at an event, your actions affect your reputation, your bookability, and your future opportunities. Don't let a lack of professionalism be the reason you stop getting booked.

Professional courtesy

One clear sign that ego is creeping in is when a speaker starts treating others as if they're simply there to serve them: barking orders, making unnecessary demands, or delegating things you really shouldn't. It's not a good look, and trust me, word gets around.

Take the case of a leading economist who was utterly exhausted from jet lag. Fair enough, it happens. Her contract, agreed in advance, included a VIP dinner after her speech, but as she was being driven from the venue, she decided she was too tired to attend. She called the bureau office to ask if she could skip it – a perfectly reasonable request under normal circumstances. Well, it would have been reasonable except for the fact that the client was sitting right next to her in the chauffeured car, listening to the entire conversation. That's how to make an awkward situation even more uncomfortable. A little foresight, and the whole thing could have been handled with far more grace.

I've mentioned this before but it's worth repeating: briefing calls are often the first time a client speaks directly to a speaker, and they want reassurance. This is the chance to know that the speaker has been properly briefed, understands the event, and is happy to do it. Handing them off to someone else can make it seem like you think you're too important to handle the client yourself. If a client is investing in you, they want to feel like you value the opportunity, not that you're above the basics of preparation.

There's also the matter of basic professional courtesy. One UK politician we occasionally booked had a habit of calling the bureau, issuing vague, one-line instructions without introducing himself and then hanging up, clearly expecting things to magically happen. The thing is that our phone line wasn't a direct line for him; whoever picked up had to work out who he was, which of the forty people in the office might be expecting this information, and what on earth needed to be done. Withheld number, of course. Completely unnecessary, utterly unhelpful, and just plain rude.

Respect the clock

At a recent event, I watched a keynote speaker refuse to cut his material to account for a technical delay. It was disappointing because he's an outstanding speaker, but in that moment, he became 'the timing guy' – the speaker who put himself above the event.

This wasn't just any event. Every speaker was on a tightly controlled schedule, with the day running to the minute, and he wasn't just any speaker – he was the first speaker of the day. When his microphone and clicker failed and had to be reset, instead of adapting like a pro, he insisted on restarting his speech as if nothing had happened. The result? He overran, throwing off the entire agenda before the day had even properly begun.

The real damage wasn't just the extra minutes. The knock-on effect was immediate and significant. Organisers weren't listening to his talk anymore; they were scrambling to fix the schedule. Other speakers were pulled aside and asked to trim their time. The backstage team was frantically checking where minutes could be shaved off upcoming sessions.

Instead of enjoying the content, everyone involved in the event was distracted, talking, problem solving, and working around the disruption he'd caused, and of course, these things get noticed. When organisers are rushing around, whispering in corners, speaking to other presenters, and checking the agenda, audience members start paying attention to that instead of the speaker. We're naturally curious and it's human nature to wonder what's going wrong, so now, instead of engaging with his message, everyone was looking for clues about what was happening behind the scenes.

What did people remember from the event? Not his talk. Not his insights. Just the headache he created. A single speaker's decision to prioritise himself over the flow of the day left an impression, but not the kind any speaker wants. It would have been so easy to drop an anecdote or trim a few minutes, but instead, his ego took centre stage, and that's the real problem. No one remembers the great content when it comes packaged with a bad experience. As speakers, we don't just deliver talks, we help shape events; the most-booked speakers leave organisers with positive memories, not logistical nightmares.

Stop talking

One of the most common challenges I've noticed when working with speakers is that they just keep talking. Whether it's an introductory call, a consultation, or a briefing for an event, some speakers treat every question as an invitation to launch into a long-winded speech. Instead of answering directly, they go off on tangents, turning what should be a conversation into a monologue.

If you do this to me, I will interrupt you and tell you to stop. I want useful information, not a performance. When I ran my bureau, I often had to ask the same question multiple times just to get a straight answer. Now, in my consulting work, I still find myself steering conversations back on track when a speaker talks in circles instead of answering the question.

One speaker stands out in my memory. She is talented but had a habit of talking too much. A client was interested in booking her but wanted a bit more information before making a final decision. My bureau colleague, knowing her tendency to ramble, explicitly told her to keep it brief. When the client asked her a simple question, 'What's your story?', she gave the full forty-five minute version. She didn't get the job and she didn't get any more work from my colleague. To her credit, she's since learned her lesson, but it was an expensive lesson.

What causes this behaviour? Sometimes it's ego – the need to be centre stage, to keep the spotlight on yourself, but often it's the opposite – a lack of confidence. Some speakers over-talk because they're trying to prove their worth. Regardless of the reason, it comes across the same way, as self-absorbed and unaware of the listener's needs.

Briefing calls and client meetings are not the time for a mini keynote. They're a chance to understand the client's needs, gather details, and show that you're there to serve the event, not just yourself. A speaker who listens well doesn't just make a better impression, they gain valuable insights that help them deliver a better talk.

If you find yourself talking more than listening, stop and ask yourself whether you're answering the question. Are you giving the client what they need to do their job? Or are you talking for the sake of it? Talking too much might feel like showcasing your expertise, but often it signals that you're not paying attention.

As a speaker, your job is to engage, not dominate. Sometimes, the most powerful thing you can do is say less and listen more.

Staying in check

I'll be honest: I know I can be direct, impatient, and sometimes a bit prickly. It's just how I am. I also know that self-awareness is important and so I do my best to manage the rough edges. No one's perfect. We're all human.

Ego creeps in when you lose sight of your flaws, and that's why feedback is so important. It helps keep you in check. My colleague Mary Tillson-Wharton has a brilliant (and slightly terrifying) exercise for speakers. She suggests asking family, friends, customers, and clients one simple question: 'What's it like being on the receiving end of me?' The answers can be eye-opening, sometimes uncomfortable, but always valuable. It takes guts to ask and, for the record, I haven't quite worked up the courage to do it myself yet (don't tell Mary), but I've seen the impact it has had on others.

It's not easy to hear how others experience you, but if you don't know, how can you improve? The same applies in your professional life. Are you actively asking clients for feedback after an event, or do you only hear it when someone forces it on you? Proactively seeking feedback shows humility and a willingness to grow. It also stops you from assuming everything's fine when there might be small issues holding you back.

Mary also has a great approach for getting real feedback on a speech. She suggests asking three times. The first time, you'll get a polite but generic response; the second time, you'll get a little more depth, but it's the third time that really matters. That's when you get the good, the bad, and the ugly. That's when people tell you what really worked, what didn't, and what could be better.

Feedback isn't an attack, it's a gift. It gives you the chance to adjust, improve, and ultimately become a better speaker. The goal isn't perfection, it's progress.

Don't take yourself too seriously

I know I said I wouldn't name names in this chapter, to protect my professional reputation and spare a few blushes, but I'll make an exception for former 400m runner Roger Black, whose career spans European, Commonwealth, World Championship, and Olympic success. Like many retired athletes, Roger transitioned to speaking after his active track career had, naturally, faded a little. For some, this could have been a blow to their ego, but Roger? He managed to handle it with humour and charm, a perfect example of not taking yourself too seriously.

The first time I worked with Roger in a professional setting, we had a briefing meeting with two client representatives. It was going well and we all ordered coffees. Roger, clearly hungry, added a bacon sandwich to his order. The coffees arrived promptly, but as the meeting carried on, the sandwich didn't. After quite a while, I offered to chase it up, but Roger said he'd handle it himself.

He called over the young waitress who had taken the original order. He started his sentence with, 'Do you know who…' and I cringed, sinking slightly into my seat, fearing he might finish with, 'I am?' Instead, with a cheeky grin, he finished, '…who I used to be?' The clients and I burst out laughing, charmed by his ability to make light of the situation. The waitress, however, wasn't fazed. She simply looked at him blankly and replied, 'No idea'. She had the last word, but the moment perfectly summed up Roger's attitude.

It's hard to let your ego ruin your speaking career when you don't take yourself too seriously. Roger's ability to laugh at himself not only saved the moment but also left a lasting impression of his humility and good humour. If more speakers adopted that kind of mindset, they'd find ego much less of a stumbling block.

Signs your ego might be getting in the way

If you're wondering whether ego is holding you back, take a moment to reflect. The first and most obvious sign? Are you still getting booked? If your bookings are dropping off, it's easy to blame external factors such as the industry, the economy, even AI, but sometimes the issue is closer to home.

Another clue is how you interact with others in the industry. Do you find yourself clashing with event organisers, clients, or support teams more than you used to? It's unlikely that they've *all* changed overnight, so it might be worth checking if something in your approach needs adjusting. Have you become less flexible? More defensive about feedback? Resistant to tailoring your content? A 'my way or the highway' attitude is a red flag.

Then there's your content. When was the last time you genuinely learned something new? If your talk is 90% the same as it was three years or even one year ago, you might be coasting. The most-booked speakers stay curious, constantly improving and refining, keeping their material fresh.

Your promotional materials can also reveal a lot. Look at your website and social media. Is it all about you? Your achievements? Your story? If your marketing is too self-focused, it might be time to reconnect with why you started speaking in the first place.

A good question to ask yourself is: 'Do you still enjoy speaking?' A lot of bad behaviour comes from boredom – with your content, hotel living, or the job itself. Sometimes it's not that you don't love speaking anymore, it's that you've gotten too busy or maybe tired of all the travel. If that's the case, take time out. You may just need a break or you may need to step back and reassess what excites you.

A hugely successful speaker I worked with delivered the exact same talk, word for word, for years. I'd seen him many times before do a fantastic job, but on one occasion, it was painfully obvious that he was bored, tired, or distracted (or perhaps all three). He had delivered it so often that he had switched to autopilot. He was in the room but he wasn't. The energy was gone, the delivery was flat, and you could see people disengaging. The truth is you have to be in the moment.

If you've done a talk too many times and you're just going through the motions, it's time for a refresh.

Your client relationships are another strong indicator. Are you getting repeat bookings? Are clients recommending you? If not, something isn't working. Strong client relationships are built on professionalism, adaptability, and humility, qualities that ego can quickly undermine.

When was the last time you watched another speaker? Sitting in the audience and observing others is a great reality check. It gives you perspective, helps you refine your own delivery, and can even highlight things you might want to avoid.

Beyond that, having a supportive peer group makes all the difference. The speaking industry is competitive but many speakers are happy to share their ups and downs. Staying connected with others keeps your ego in check and reminds you that, no matter how experienced you are, there's always something new to learn.

If any of these signs feel familiar, it's not the end of the world; it just means it's time to take stock. Speaking is a craft, and like any craft, it needs constant attention, improvement, and self-awareness.

Be grateful

After all these years in the speaking industry, I can honestly say it's a privilege to work in this space. Speaking for a living opens doors – to travel, learning, meeting incredible people, and making a good living while doing something meaningful. It's easy to get caught up in the challenges but there's a lot to be grateful for.

As already mentioned, one of the best ways to keep ego in check is to revisit why you started speaking in the first place. What made you step onto that stage? What did you love about it in the beginning? Finding joy in what you do today helps stop ego from creeping in.

Another way to stay grounded is giving back. How can you support speakers just starting out? Could you mentor someone, speak to students, or share your experiences in a way that helps others? Engaging with those at the beginning of their journey reminds you where you came from, what you've achieved, and what's still possible.

Writing this book has done the same for me. It's reminded me why I love working with speakers like you, so thank you – consider my ego checked.

Ego: Action points

I have summarised ten action points that you can turn to if you suspect your ego is creeping up on you.

1. **'Be a diva onstage but a delight offstage.'** Of course, you must deliver an outstanding performance on stage, but the minute your speaking role ends, shift the spotlight to clients and organisers.

2. **Celebrate healthy confidence.** Enjoy the confidence you get from preparation, practice, and repetition. Avoid slipping into arrogance by staying adaptable and receptive to feedback.

3. **Keep listening.** Always be ready to tailor your material and delivery. 'I know best' thinking and behaviour seriously undermines your bookability.

4. **Foster team spirit.** Don't get hung up on titles, seniority, or your status. Join the wider event team and work together to ensure success overall.

5. **Stay classy.** Always be professional. Avoid inappropriate relationships, drunkenness, rudeness, and other misdemeanours. There are few quicker ways to damage your reputation and reduce future bookings.

6. **Avoid unnecessary delegation.** Handle client meetings, briefing calls, and groundwork yourself.

7. **Conversation is two-way.** Don't fall into on-stage habits in your day-to-day conversations. Fight the temptation to answer client questions with one-way performative monologues. It's rude.

8. **Don't be afraid of feedback.** Actively seek the opinion of others and regularly evaluate your behaviour. If you've deviated from professional expectations, be quick to make the necessary corrections.

9. **Park your vanity.** Ensure all your activities, including self-promotion, emphasise the value you bring. Even if you're wildly successful, it's never about you; it's always about the results of your work.

10. **Embrace gratitude and humour.** Appreciate everything a speaking career offers and maintain a sense of humour. Light-heartedness and generosity go a long way in keeping your ego in check.

Conclusion

Here we are, the end of the book, so of course I want to leave you with something useful, practical, and inspiring. The speaking world is full of amazing opportunities, and everything I've shared in this book is designed to help you make the most of them.

This is just the beginning. The Bookability Formula gives you a solid foundation, but success as a speaker doesn't happen overnight. Building a profitable, sustainable speaking business takes time, effort, and continuous growth. The world moves fast, client needs change, industries shift, new trends emerge, and audience expectations evolve. If you want to stay bookable, you have to keep up, adapt, and refine what you do.

Feeling motivated? Great... but motivation alone isn't enough. If you're new to speaking, you should know that there are very few barriers to entry in this industry. Anyone can call themselves a speaker, but the ones who succeed? They put in the work. That starts now. If you haven't already, take time to go back through the stories and strategies I've shared and figure out how they apply to you.

You might have noticed that this book isn't full of celebrity case studies. That's because this isn't about household names. It's about hardworking, professional speakers. Everything I've covered applies whether you're just starting out, trying to establish yourself, breaking into a new market, or pushing for higher fees. That's the real power of The Bookability Formula: every variable works together to create a blueprint for long-term success.

$$B = \frac{(R+K+M+E)^V}{e}$$

Each variable of this formula matters and has a key role in your overall bookability:

- Being relevant (R) gets your foot in the door.
- Being known (K) makes sure the right people remember you in the right way.
- Being memorable (M) keeps you at the top of their shortlist.

CONCLUSION

- Being easy to book and work with (E) makes sure they book you again.
- Adding value (V) turns clients into long-term advocates.
- Finally, of course, there's ego (e). Left unchecked, it undoes everything.

To be relevant (R), you need to truly understand your audience, what challenges they face, and what problems they need solving. It's not enough to have expertise or simply chase after the latest trend; you have to position yourself as essential. A bookable speaker isn't just interesting; they're needed.

To be known (K), you must make sure the right people know who you are and what you do. It's not about ego or self-promotion; it's about visibility in a competitive market. The difference between a struggling speaker and a booked-out speaker is that the latter makes a consistent effort to be seen and remembered.

To be memorable (M), you need to stand out in a crowded industry. That means having strong positioning, a compelling message, and a distinct voice. It also means staying in touch with bookers, sending the occasional well-chosen gift, and making sure you don't just get remembered, but recommended.

To be easy to work with (E), you need to remove friction for the people who book you. I've seen speakers lose jobs, not because they weren't great on stage, but because they were difficult behind the scenes. Bookers will pick a speaker who is easy to deal with over someone who is a headache, even if they're slightly less impressive on stage.

To increase your value (V), you must go beyond just delivering a great talk. When clients see you as an investment rather than an expense, your fees go up, your demand increases, and you build a reputation for being someone who truly delivers results.

Finally, there's ego (e). Unchecked, ego is the thing that will quietly erode your bookability. It's the speaker who stops listening, stops learning, and starts believing they're the most important person in the room. It's the one who demands special treatment, ignores feedback, and assumes they don't need to improve. It can be career-ending, but when ego is in check, when you approach speaking with humility, professionalism, and a focus on the client, you become the speaker who gets booked again and again.

At the end of the day, a successful speaking career isn't about the applause you get on stage. It's about the impact you have on the bookers and clients who trust you with their event.

It's never about you, and neither is it about quick wins which risk fleeting success. It's about ongoing targeted hard work. Consistency drives success, and The

CONCLUSION

Bookability Formula isn't something you master once and forget, it requires ongoing attention. By consistently focusing on these principles and applying them in your speaking business, you'll start to see small, incremental improvements, and, over time, these will add up. Every action you take, even the ones that feel insignificant in the moment, moves you forward. Keep putting in the effort and you'll see the results.

The speaking industry is full of opportunities and success follows a simple rule: work consistently and the rewards will come. The demand for insight, inspiration, education, and challenge will always be there. People will always look to experts, thought leaders, and storytellers to help them navigate change, spark ideas, and drive action. That's why there will always be a place for speakers like you, whether it's in corporate boardrooms, on the world's biggest stages, or in today's ever-growing virtual spaces.

One speaker who embodies this is Luc Colemont, a leading gastroenterologist who, at the time of writing, has delivered over a thousand keynotes on preventing colorectal cancer. His mission? To save lives, one speaking engagement at a time.

Your goals don't have to be as dramatic as Colemont's, but why not aim high? What kind of impact do you want to make? Decide on the legacy you want to leave then go out and make it happen.

Before I go, I want to say thank you. Thank you for reading, for investing in your growth, and for making it to the end of this book. It's been a pleasure to share The Bookability Formula with you and the greatest gift you can give me in return is your success.

That said, I'm still learning too. The speaking industry evolves constantly, and I'm always looking at what's working, what's changing, and how speakers can stay ahead. To be honest, it's been hard to stop adding to this book.

If you want to keep up with what I'm seeing in the market, how The Bookability Formula continues to apply, and the latest insights on getting booked and staying booked, I'd love for you to follow me on social media or check out my website. Just search for Maria Franzoni or follow the links given below and you'll find me.

Here's to your bookable future.

Maria

> **TIP**
>
> If you'd like all the action points and tips in one list, go to my website: www.mariafranzoni.me/bookability

Recommended Reading

There is always more to learn to help build your speaking careers. The following books are favourites of mine, full of strategies, tools, and inspiration to help you grow a thriving business.

Jones, Phil M, *Exactly What to Say: The magic words for influence and impact* (Box of Tricks Books, 2017)

Persuasion is at the heart of every great speaking business and this book is a toolkit for using the right words to influence and engage. It's perfect for crafting pitches, negotiating fees, and connecting with audiences.

Keller, Gary and Jay Papasan, *The One Thing: The surprisingly simple truth about extraordinary results* (Bard Press, 2013)

Speakers often juggle multiple priorities but this book teaches the importance of focusing on what truly matters. By identifying and concentrating on your most impactful activities, you can achieve greater results in less time.

Koch, Richard, *The 80/20 Principle: The secret of achieving more with less* (Nicholas Brealey Publishing, 2022)

This book reveals how a small percentage of your efforts produce most of your results. For speakers, this book can unlock enormous potential, helping you focus on the highest-value activities that drive bookings, revenue, and long-term success. This principle is what originally led me to develop The Bookability Formula.

Michalowicz, Mike, *Profit First: Transform your business from a cash-eating monster to a money-making machine (Entrepreneurship simplified)* (Portfolio, 2017)

Managing finances effectively is crucial for building a sustainable speaking business. This book introduces a cash management system that ensures profitability from day one. It helps speakers take control of their income, allocate funds wisely, and avoid the common pitfalls that lead to financial stress. Do what I did and buy a copy for your accountant.

RECOMMENDED READING

Newman, David, *Do It! Speaking: 77 instant-action ideas to market, monetize, and maximize your expertise* (HarperCollins Publishers, 2017)

An essential guide for speakers looking to build their business, this book covers everything from marketing to performance. It's filled with practical advice to help you get booked, grow your income, and make the most of your expertise.

Nihill, David, *Do You Talk Funny?: Seven comedy habits to become a better (and funnier) public speaker* (BenBella Books, 2016)

Humour is one of the most powerful tools a speaker can have. This book breaks down how comedians structure stories, engage audiences, and make people laugh, providing practical techniques you can apply to your own talks. Whether you're naturally funny or not, this book helps you use humour to connect, entertain, and be memorable, a key ingredient in bookability.

Port, Michael and Andrew Davis, *The Referable Speaker: Your guide to building a sustainable speaking career—no fame required* (Page Two Press, 2021)

This book focuses on what makes a speaker memorable and marketable. It provides actionable advice on crafting a unique style and ensuring that your message sticks with audiences and decision-makers alike.

Priestley, Daniel, *Key Person of Influence: The five-step method to become one of the most highly valued and highly paid people in your industry* (Rethink Press, 3rd edition, 2014)

This book outlines the steps to becoming a highly valued and sought-after expert in your industry. For speakers, it provides a framework to establish credibility, create valuable assets, and position yourself as the go-to authority, making it easier to attract opportunities and charge higher fees.

Schaefer, Mark W, *Known: The handbook for building and unleashing your personal brand in the digital age* (Shaefer Marketing Solutions, 2017)

This practical guide offers a clear roadmap to building a personal brand. Speakers can learn how to define their niche, connect with the right audiences, and position themselves as the leading experts in their field.

Voss, Chris and Tahl Raz, *Never Split the Difference: Negotiating As If Your Life Depended On It* (Harper Business, 2016)

A masterclass in negotiation, this book shares techniques from a former FBI hostage negotiator. It's particularly useful for speakers negotiating contracts, fees, and terms, helping you approach every conversation with confidence and strategy.

Acknowledgements

This book, and the work it is based on, would not exist without the following incredible individuals, to whom I am deeply grateful:

Alex Krywald, who took a chance on me back in 1998 and saw something in me that I didn't see in myself.

Allison Grenfell, who provided the original data from that 2019 conference that set this journey in motion.

Audrey Shaw and Sian Jones, for their unwavering support and loyalty, even when I came up with hare-brained ideas!

Beth Sherman, for her invaluable feedback and input.

Brendan Hall, for not only providing insightful feedback but also contributing additional stories.

David Newman, for his incredible generosity in providing feedback on my first draft. I am forever indebted.

David Sellars, for his endless patience, calm presence, and tolerance of my 'just five more minutes' that somehow lasted a year.

Dominic Eldred Earl, who first suggested that I might be good at mentoring and coaching speakers.

James Taylor, for both his thoughtful feedback and the additional examples of the Bookability Formula in action.

Jamil Qureshi, for so much, primarily for the second chance to say yes to working with him, for his trust, and for his constant encouragement to pursue this work.

Mary Tillson-Wharton, who has helped me untangle my thinking and articulate it coherently, and who fills in the areas I can't help speakers with.

Richard Koch, for laying the foundation of everything Mary and I share, and for your enthusiasm when I told you about this book.

ACKNOWLEDGEMENTS

Tom Kenyon-Slaney and Brendan O'Connor, for giving me the freedom to open my own bureau while still allowing me to be part of a larger organisation.

I am also forever indebted to the bookable speakers whose stories and wisdom have helped illustrate the Bookability Formula in action. Some I have already mentioned, but also the following:

Adah Parris; Dr Alison Edgar MBE; Andrew Davis; Anna Hemmings MBE; Beau Lotto; Beth Sherman; Sir Bob Geldof; Brad Burton; Brendan Hall; Bruno Marion; David Avrin; Elin Hauge; Captain Emma Henderson MBE; Felicity Ashley; Gavin Ingham; Graham Allcott; Holly Budge; James Taylor; Jaz Ampaw-Farr; Jonas Ridderstråle; Ken Hughes; Sir Ken Robinson; Kjell A. Nordström; Lawrie McMenemy MBE; Lee Warren; Dr Luc Colemont; Mark Leruste; Mark Stevenson; Martin Lindstrom; Neil Armstrong; Paul Adamson; Paul Boross MBE; Paul McKenna; Penny Mallory; Philip Hesketh; Sir Ranulph Fiennes; Ricardo Cabete; Robin Sieger; Roger Black MBE; Rohit Talwar; Ross Bernstein; Sarah Furness; and Dame Stephanie Shirley.

The Author

Maria Franzoni is one of the most trusted names in the speaking industry. Since 1998, she has worked at the heart of the industry, first booking speakers for audiences around the world, and more recently supporting them to build thriving speaking businesses. Over the years, she has booked thousands of speakers, shaped the careers of countless experts and thought leaders, and worked with some of the most celebrated names, including Neil Armstrong, Richard Branson, Bear Grylls, Anita Roddick and Bob Geldof.

As a former speaker bureau owner and agent, Maria understands exactly what it takes to get booked, and rebooked. Today, she helps speakers become the most bookable in their field by applying the proven tactics used by the industry's top performers. She also works with speaker bureaus, helping their agents grow successful rosters and book smarter.

Maria is the creator of The Bookability Formula, a practical framework based on what the top 1% of speakers consistently do to stay in demand. She hosts the long-running Speaking Business podcast, where she shares insider knowledge, smart strategies and real-world stories from the industry.

She lives in the UK with her husband David and their labradoodle Oscar, Coton de Tulear Teddie, and their Maine Coon cat Coco, and continues to help the next generation of speakers and bookers succeed in an ever-changing market.

🌐 www.mariafranzoni.me

in www.linkedin.com/in/mariafranzoni